CULTOGRAPHIES

CULTOGRAPHIES is a new list of individual studies devoted to the analysis of cult film. The series provides a comprehensive introduction to those films which have attained the coveted status of a cult classic, focusing on their particular appeal, the ways in which they have been conceived, constructed and received, and their place in the broader popular cultural landscape. For more information, please visit www.cultographies.com

Series editors: Ernest Mathijs (University of British Columbia) and Jamie Sexton (University of Wales, Aberystwyth)

OTHER PUBLISHED TITLES IN THE CULTOGRAPHIES SERIES

COMING SOON!

Bad Taste

Jim Barratt

WALLFLOWER PRESS
LONDON & NEW YORK

First published in Great Britain in 2008 by
Wallflower Press
6 Market Place, London W1W 8AF
www.wallflowerpress.co.uk

A catalogue record for this book is available from the British Library.

ISBN 978-1-905674-87-9 (pbk)

Series design by Elsa Mathern

Printed and bound in Poland; produced by Polskabook

CONTENTS

ACKNOWLEDGEMENTS

I'd like to thank the following for giving so freely and generously of their time and sharing their memories of *Bad Taste*: Ken Hammon, Tony Hiles, Mike Minett, Lindsay Shelton and Craig Smith.

Special thanks to Hamish Towgood for lots of help along the way, and to Lewis Davies & Pete Gunter, Thomas Hartlage and Jake West, for their personal testimonies of the film's significance.

I'm very grateful to David Steele and Donna Payne for providing insights into all things Kiwi and making many helpful contributions to the text.

Thanks are also due to the following for their kind assistance of one sort or another: Andrew Button, Grace Carley, Joseph D'Morais, Matthew Dravitzki, Kathleen Drumm, Jane Giles, Mladen Ivancic, Stefan Jaworzyn, Pete Johnson, Alan Jones, Steve Jones, Marc Morris, Nick and Jo Roddick, Tony Timpone and the staff of the British Film Institute library.

Finally, I'm indebted to the series editors, Ernest Mathijs and Jamie Sexton, for their sagely guidance, and to Yoram Allon of Wallflower Press for this wonderful opportunity to work through my nerdy depravity in print.

This book is dedicated to Catherine, for her impeccable good taste. And to Dylan, Tudor and Arianne, as proof of the above.

PROLOGUE

On a late summer's day in February 1882 a full-rigged sailing ship left the docks of Port Chalmers in New Zealand. The ship, the *Dunedin*, was unremarkable except for one fact: it carried a cargo of animal carcasses housed in chambers chilled by a steam powered Bell-Coleman freezing plant. This was the first refrigerated shipment of meat ever to leave New Zealand shores bound for London, on the other side of the world.

In less than one hundred days the *Dunedin* was berthed on the Thames and all but one of its nearly 5,000 carcasses of mutton, lamb and pork had been passed fit for sale at a price nearly double what they would have made back home. 'From a purely technical perspective', notes historian James Belich, 'refrigeration was the knight in icy armour that rode to the rescue of the New Zealand economy in the 1880s' (2001: 54). Within a short period the fortunes of the ailing economy were reversed, and an industry was born whose scale and importance had a profound impact on almost every aspect of New Zealand life. Farming, and the rural landscape upon which it thrived, was transformed and meat works sprung up everywhere.

'It is difficult to realise that only about thirty-five years have elapsed since one of the most important of the world's industries was inaugurated, resulting in the enormous and increasing trade of the present day', wrote M.A. Elliott in the *New Zealand Journal of Science and Technology* in 1918. 'And yet the whole of this great industry, and to a very great extent the general prosperity and advancement of New Zealand, hangs on the slender piston rod of a refrigerating machine' (1918). From tiny acorns, mighty oaks grow.

***

James Gear was one of those whose personal fortune was made by the burgeoning meat industry. Originally from Somerset in England, Gear had a successful business in the butchers' trade, serving the local market around Wellington, when refrigeration made meat export a lucrative prospect. Sensing an opportunity he founded the Gear Meat Preserving and Freezing Company of New Zealand in 1882, only months after the *Dunedin*'s pioneering cargo had sold at Smithfield market. That same year he built a grand wooden colonial homestead, in the style of an Italian Palazzo, outside Porirua near the capital. A century later, Gear Homestead, as it is known today, was one of the main locations used in *Bad Taste*, doubling as the alien spaceship at the centre of Lord Crumb's *human* meat export operation.

In March 2002, one hundred and twenty years after the *Dunedin*'s trailblazing voyage, Dr Ruth Harley, CEO of the New Zealand Film Commission, gave a presentation entitled 'How we created world class performance'.[1] It was part of a three-day event led by New Zealand's Ministry of Economic Development, and the matter under consideration on that early autumn day in Christchurch was how innovation could be yoked into the service of the country's enterprise culture.

This gathering of the great and the good, comprising leading thinkers from business, politics and academia, might seem a million miles removed from the gory frivolity of *Bad Taste*, but

2

Dr Harley's speech made ample reference to it nonetheless. For in December 2000, London had played host to the world premiere of *The Fellowship of the Ring* (2001), the first film in Peter Jackson's *Lord of the Rings* trilogy. The last film in the series, *The Return of the King* (2003), would go on to win no fewer than eleven Academy Awards, including Best Picture and Best Director. The three films grossed in excess of $2.8 billion worldwide, even before sales of DVDs, merchandising and other revenue sources (Bart 2006: 52).

Little wonder, then, that Dr Harley's speech should use Jackson's career as an example of what can be achieved through innovation and enterprise. By dint of hard work, determination and natural talent nurtured by the benevolent hand of state investment (enter the New Zealand Film Commission), Jackson's is arguably the most remarkable film career in New Zealand's history, helping to elevate the national industry to, in Harley's words, 'world class performance'.[2] And it all began with *Bad Taste*. From tiny acorns, mighty, Ent-sized oaks grow.

***

The themes of enterprise and meat export are not the only sinuous links between the *Dunedin* and *Bad Taste*. In their own way each story exemplifies, and helps to perpetuate, mythical aspects of the national character of New Zealanders: the qualities of self-reliance, tenacity and, perhaps above all, the have-a-go ingenuity that sees every problem as a challenge to be overcome with a bit of common sense and some Number 8 fencing wire.

The economic miracle that followed in the wake of the *Dunedin* came about because there was a strong demand, an *appetite*, for New Zealand meat among those queuing at butchers' slabs the length and breadth of Mother Britain. That is the essence of benign business enterprise: catering to demand in a way that promotes mutual benefit. And it is a quality that has shone through in Jackson's career, beginning with his cult debut.

'Something worth mentioning is the status that some films have as "cult films"', Jackson wrote in a letter to the New Zealand Film Commission seeking investment for *Bad Taste*.

> A cult film, particularly a cheap one, often becomes a huge financial success due to the repeat viewings from a group of hard-core fans. While I would be reluctant to make any such claims about *Giles* being 'cult material' [*Giles' Big Day*, which would become *Bad Taste*] I think it contains many of the elements of the cult film and it stands up well to repeat viewing. Only time will tell … (quoted in Sibley 2006: 94).

To understand the cult of *Bad Taste* you have to cast your eye wider than the film itself. That's the reason this book, in addition to looking at the film's production and distribution history, also voices the testimony of fans like Hamish Towgood, a Kiwi who saw the film when he was 13 and went on to set up the Ultimate Bad Taste website; and Jake West, a young British director whose second feature, *Evil Aliens* (2005), is a 'love letter' to 'old school horror' like *Bad Taste*. Then there's Thomas Hartlage, who runs two German record labels and befriended Peter Jackson on a trip to New Zealand before organising and distributing the official *Bad Taste* soundtrack album; and the legion of fans that contribute to fanzines or participate in online bulletin boards and review sites, attend festival screenings and conventions. Every one of them has found something special in *Bad Taste*, some quality worthy of reverence, and it is my task to understand quite what makes *Bad Taste*, a quintessentially New Zealand film, an object of cult devotion the world over.

1

MY TURN FOR THE MAGNUM

Context may justify exceptions. Not the most elegant of phrases, or the most revealing when considered in isolation. But its significance lies in what it separates. For when a film censor uses the phrase, you know they are probably doing something right (although you may still disagree with certain of their decisions). The simple admission that context may justify exceptions is what separates dogmatic, knee-jerk, scissor-wielding forms of censorship from more considered and judicious approaches. The former relies on the rigid application of standards that take no account of the context within which, for example, a gory act of violence occurs in a film. If it offends against accepted standards it has to go. The latter allows for a more carefully modulated response to the same act of violence, in consideration of factors that impinge on its likely interpretation by an audience. 'Context may justify exceptions' is the difference, if you like, between hysterics and hermeneutics.

It was during my time working for the British Board of Film Classification (BBFC), for fewer than three years as the old century passed into the new, that *Bad Taste* had its greatest influence on my professional thinking. I first saw the film on video barely a decade earlier, and it had stuck with me over the years. When I took up my post at the Board, one of a dozen or so Film and Video Examiners, it was *Bad Taste*, and the films it inspired me to seek out subsequently, that marked the most extreme horizons of my film tastes. We were tasked with watching all manner of works on film and video, from arthouse to grindhouse, blockbusters to straight-to-video schlock, television serials and children's Christmas specials, Cantonese soap operas and Bollywood epics, and, of course, more pornography than you could shake a vibrating stick at. For five hours a day, three and a half days a week each team of examiners watched and noted, deliberated and discussed before recommending classifications for ratification by the management.

I don't recall whether *Bad Taste* made it into any of my examiner reports putting the case for a particular decision, or cropped up by name in discussion with colleagues (although I suspect it did), but it was always there in the back of my mind, one of the yardsticks against which to judge the steady stream of product that passed before my gaze on its way through the classification system.

The real significance of *Bad Taste*, from the perspective of film censorship, is as a textbook example of *why* context may justify exceptions. On the face of it, the basic story sits comfortably within the narrative traditions of the horror genre (or, more specifically, the science fiction horror sub-genre occupied by films like *Alien* (1979) and its sequels). We learn in the pre-title prologue that the townsfolk of Kaihoro in New Zealand, the story's fictional setting,[3] have been massacred by an unspecified force whose arrival was preceded by 'a roaring noise and a big white light in the sky'. Wasting no time, a shadowy government official calls in the Astro Investigation and Defence Service (Barry (Pete O'Herne), Frank (Mike Minett), Ozzy (Terry Potter) and Derek (Peter Jackson), known colloquially as The Boys) to deal with the phantom menace. The film follows The Boys' efforts to identify the precise nature of the threat and its source, and to deal with it decisively. It transpires the aliens, led by Lord Crumb, are on earth to gather meat samples to develop a new line of human meals for their intergalactic fast-food chain. The improvised sub-plot involves a famine relief charity collector (Giles, played by Craig Smith) who is captured by the aliens when he visits Kaihoro. The Boys mount a daring rescue in the closing stages of the film, making their escape with Giles but leaving Derek (who has become deranged following a near-fatal fall) aboard the alien spaceship, armed with a chainsaw, to settle the score with Lord Crumb.

Yet while few films can match it for gory, violent spectacle it is humour, not horror, that wins through. To their credit the joke was not lost on the British Board of Film Classification, which passed the film '18' uncut in April 1989 (well before my time, I should add).

The theatrical distributor, Blue Dolphin, appears to have anticipated some problems with the censors. According to the file, a videotape of the film was sent to James Ferman, Director of the Board at the time, for an informal view.[4] There is no record of his response, but a note indicates Ferman's thinking upon seeing the film once it had been officially submitted. He described it as 'OTT nonsense, unlikely to be taken seriously by anyone'.[5] Nonetheless the Board took a cautious approach when the film was later submitted for video classification, making sure the senior management team saw it after it had been through the usual examination process. This was a common practice at the time for films that might fall foul of the stringent 'harm' test of the Video Recordings Act of 1984. Since that legislation had come into force, video had been much more tightly controlled than films on theatrical release because of the greater likelihood of under-age viewing in the home (see Barratt 2001). But in the event this additional scrutiny was really only a formality. Margaret Ford, Deputy Director, noted the 'excess was played for humour, not for sadism', and that was the view that prevailed.[6] Just as with the theatrical version, the film was duly passed '18' uncut for video release in October 1989.

To underline the point that the context of portrayal was crucial to the film's acceptability, Guy Phelps, the Principal Examiner, wrote, 'You either accept it as fun as it is or demand cuts that would destroy it'.[7] He also suggested the film was far gorier than was usually permissible on video in a straight horror film. The fact that the humorous context justified an exception in the case of *Bad Taste* made the film such a useful point of reference during my time at the Board, helping to illustrate the simple principle that the maintenance of community standards needn't be an unthinking activity. It requires active engagement with films, just as audiences approach them.

***

I first saw *Bad Taste* at some point in 1991. I can't be more specific than that. I was in my second year at university and, like most undergraduates, too busy letting my social life get in the way of study to keep track of the calendar. It must have been during a break between semesters because I was at home. I dropped in to see a friend who worked in a local record shop and we decided to rent one of the videos stocked alongside the vinyl.

While my friend finished up I browsed the titles on display, with no particular preference in mind. *Bad Taste* was one of a number of titles I selected, purely on the strength of the lurid cover art. My friend looked over the choices and by a process of elimination we settled for *Bad Taste*. The clincher, if I recall, was the 'Gore Award' prominently displayed on the front cover. I had never heard of the Paris Festival of Fantasy and Sci-fi but the endorsement worked; we were intrigued to find out whether the film could possibly live up to its billing. The back cover offered additional enticement: 'People of a weak disposition should not watch this feature.'

Bad Taste lived up to the hyperbole, and some. Quite by chance the film came into my life at exactly the right moment to leave a lasting impression. I was open and fully receptive to its anarchic, irreverent sense of fun. Any younger and I might have dismissed it as too amateurish (younger viewers can be very unforgiving of what they perceive to be poor quality). Later in life I might never have taken a chance on it, instead settling for the safer option of a known quantity. But as it was, this random encounter in an idle moment was perfect. Here was a film that challenged my very understanding of what a film could be.

The chance manner by which I came across *Bad Taste* made the experience all the more of a pleasing surprise. Until the moment I picked up the video box I had no idea the film existed (and I liked to think at that time I was tuned in to most new releases; clearly I was wrong). I had seen no trailers or advertisements, and read no reviews. None of my friends, with their varied tastes far eclipsing mine, had ever mentioned it to me in conversation. It came with no personal recommendations, which is how I normally chose films to see. I recognised early on that an important part of the pleasure of this film was that I had discovered it for myself, and not as part of a consumer group targeted by marketers (or so I naively thought). It was like a piece of forgotten silver, passed over by others until I laid my hand on it and recognised its true worth. On viewing the film I felt, perhaps for the first time ever, like I had engaged in some sort of marginal, underground pleasure; something well beyond the safe confines of my comfortable and sheltered upbringing.

Bad Taste was not the most shocking film I had ever seen, or even the most violent (having viewed *Robocop* (1987) and *A Nightmare on Elm Street* (1984) a few years before, both of which I found enjoyable but disturbing). But it was by far the most outrageous, and one of the funniest: a wanton display of inventive, puerile mayhem.

The key to its appeal for me was that it was so unexpectedly original. H.G. Wells, and later Roald Dahl, taught us not to underestimate the power of the unexpected over our imaginations, and *Bad Taste* made such a deep impression on me precisely because it confounded my expectations. It was a film like no other I had seen, from a country I had almost no idea about.

It also introduced me to ultra-low budget, independent filmmaking. Doubtless I'd seen plenty of low-budget films, but without necessarily realising it at the time. In truth I probably never even considered they existed, such was my unfamiliarity with the actual business of film. Yet it was obvious from the very first scenes that *Bad Taste* had been made on the cheap. I was struck by the mixed quality of the acting, and the unconvincing excess of the special effects. Something was amiss. I couldn't put my finger on it, but there was also some indefinable quality that was not quite right about the sound (I had no idea, at this point, it had been added in post-production).

These were only some of the surface details that set *Bad Taste* apart from pretty much every other film I had seen. At a deeper level I found it hard to place in genre terms, for it appeared to straddle horror, science fiction, action and the combat movie, with a strong dose of comedy. The lack of a clear generic pedigree can be disorientating for audiences, forcing them to work harder to make sense of a narrative without the guiding hand of convention. Added to this, the narrative elements of plot and story appeared thrown together in a rather cavalier fashion, with little regard for traditional notions of structure, continuity or characterisation. Nothing much about the film seemed to conform to received wisdom.

That is not to say the film didn't work. On the contrary, none of these apparent flaws seemed to matter because it hung together perfectly well, carried along by a gleeful energy that made compelling viewing. I don't think of *Bad Taste* as a good 'bad film', that perverse category of cult movies that are so truly awful as to be entertaining (films like Edward D. Wood Jr's *Plan 9 From Outer Space* (1959)). I'm not alone in thinking that *Bad Taste* is well crafted, despite budgetary shortcomings, with interesting and dynamic camerawork, sharp editing and adroitly choreographed special effects set pieces. As Costa Botes told Jackson's biographer: 'You often see amateur films that look amateur, play amateur and don't go beyond the obvious. But *Bad Taste* is not like that and I could tell, even from the very early rough-cut, that it was clearly the work of a well-developed talent' (quoted in Sibley 2006: 113–14). Beneath its cut-price outward appearance I recognised what others have discerned: *Bad Taste* was born out of a passion for cinema and for filmmaking, and it speaks directly to those who share such enthusiasms.

If anything, the low-budget sensibility heightened my pleasure in the film. It was part of the overall joke, a cry of take-it-or-leave-it defiance by the filmmakers. It felt wilfully perverse to find gratification in something most likely to be decried by the majority, and I exalted in this minor act of rebellion.

After that first viewing *Bad Taste* surfaced in conversation any time the subject of film favourites came up in my presence. At university I can remember proselytising the film's virtues to anyone that would listen, hoping to win converts to the faith. The fact that I was almost alone in having seen the film marked me out as having wayward and adventurous tastes, which was partly the effect I wanted to achieve by expressing my passion for it.[8] I've no doubt it was also dismissed by less charitable souls as evidence of nerdy depravity, but that was something I could live with. The expression of taste is a matter of social distinction, as Pierre Bourdieu (1986) has described, and marginal tastes can bring social cachet in the right circumstances – what Matt Hills calls 'subcultural distinctiveness' in his account of horror fandom (2005: 85).

What strikes me now is actually how little I knew about the film I was so fond of discussing. Almost everything I had to say about it was gleaned from that first encounter, because I had never bothered to follow up my interest with further enquiry (this was a time before the Internet helped bring together communities of interest, expediting the circulation of fan knowledge). I remember telling people the film was so cheap and reckless the filmmakers used real animal entrails in the special effects, because that's exactly what it looked like on screen. It was only later I discovered this was true. I knew the film hailed from New Zealand, but I had no idea it was a debut feature or that it had been shot over the course of four years. It was little surprise to discover the principal cast and crew were amateurs, but at the time I had no firm evidence this was the case. In other words, I had no inkling of quite what a remarkable achievement *Bad Taste* actually was. Had I known, it probably would have only further increased my admiration and enthusiasm.

***

Before seeing *Bad Taste* I had limited exposure to screen representations of New Zealand. I watched a few episodes of *Children of Fire Mountain* (1981) when it was televised in the early 1980s, but it left me largely unmoved. I can only recall bafflement at the unfamiliar historical setting (the 1900s), foreign location (complete with volcano) and the depiction of Maori life. Other than that I was dimly aware of New Zealand from news reports of Royal visits, rugby and cricket tours and the like but I had no sense of kinship with the most distant member of our shared Commonwealth.

That changed with *Bad Taste*, which recast the American genre films I was most familiar with and gave them a distinctive Kiwi flavour. 'It's a very Kiwi film with a very Kiwi feel – basically a Kiwi film about Kiwi jokers' is how Jackson once described it (Pryor 2003: 36). It felt fresh and different, while at the same time much of the setting, the *mise-en-scène* and dialogue were comfortingly familiar. Images of a green and pleasant land and everyday objects and experiences that were common to Britain (the Morris Minor, a Charles and Di wristwatch and so on) helped forge in me a connection to a 'foreign' film that I had never before felt. *Bad Taste* contained an invigorating mix of the recognisable and the exotic, a winning combination in a cult film (and possibly why it has a stronger following overseas than at home).

***

Watching *Bad Taste* for the first time was less an epiphany and more of a watershed moment in the formation of my film tastes. It brought together two modes of cinematic expression, gore and humour, to which I had been ineluctably drawn for some time. Whereas previously I had expressed no particular preference for one type of film over another, I became much more inclined to seek out horror films, particularly if they had comedy elements. In this way I came eventually to watch all those movies most frequently cited in connection with *Bad Taste*, either as sources of inspiration or as fellow travellers along the road to comic excess: *Dawn of the Dead* (1978), *The Evil Dead* (1982) and *Evil Dead II* (1987), *The Return of the Living Dead* (1984), *Re-Animator* (1985) and so on. By the time I joined the British Board of Film Classification I had watched enough 'video nasties' (and I use that term as a mark of distinction rather than opprobrium) to put me in good stead for the task at hand. As I was to discover, there was very little that could shock or surprise me. My exposure to countless imaginary horrors had made me more aware of the techniques employed by filmmakers to achieve their effects, and less susceptible to their emotional impact. Better able, therefore, to consider them dispassionately and in context.

Later I had the enormous satisfaction of seeing *Braindead* (1992), Jackson's zombie comedy, which demonstrated how much the director could achieve given a larger budget and the benefit of a professional cast and crew. When the critical buzz that greeted *Heavenly Creatures* (1994) drew my attention to Jackson's involvement I leaped at the chance of seeing the film on the big screen. I was not disappointed. Here was demonstration that Jackson was a prodigious and versatile talent, in terms that even those outside the usual fan circle of his splatter movies could appreciate. By definition, cult films inspire a very deep personal investment by fans, and in the critical acclaim of *Heavenly Creatures* I felt the warm glow of reflected glory. It was a sensation that was to be repeated with the success of the *Lord of the Rings* trilogy, and a reminder that the cult of *Bad Taste* is now bound up with Peter Jackson's status as one of the leading filmmakers of his generation.

2

WEEKEND COWBOYS

'I always say that [*Bad Taste*] is Peter Jackson's film but if he had made it with a different group of people it would be a different movie' (Ken Hammon 2001).

'We were *all* oddball, nerdy fan-boys, hanging out together, going to movies and then trying to *make* a movie' (Craig Smith, quoted in Sibley 2006: 83; emphasis in original).

Makara is home to Wellington's main cemetery and lies to the west of the city, only about twenty minutes drive from the centre. At weekends the local beach and coastal walks attract visitors to the area, but during the week, when there's no one around, the township 'is quite a creepy, desolate sort of place', according to Craig Smith, who plays Giles Copeland, the charity collector, in *Bad Taste*.[9] This made it an ideal location for the short film Jackson and his collaborators, including Ken Hammon, Pete O'Herne and Smith, had planned to make. The eerie quiet of the area was 'just perfect for the tone of the piece'.[10]

Principal photography got underway on 27 October 1983, four days before Jackson's twenty-second birthday. Accounts vary as to the intended length of the short film, which is given as either ten or twenty minutes, but it is of little consequence.[11] The film, originally called *Roast of the Day*, was meant to provide an opportunity to put Jackson's newly acquired 16mm Bolex camera through its paces, resulting in a short that could gain some festival exposure, and maybe lead to work in the film industry. In the event the production, originally scheduled for one month, stretched to over four years, went through numerous title and plot changes, saw cast and crew come and go (and return again), and grew to full feature length. It was, in the words of the Beatles (one of Jackson's favourite bands), a long and winding road.

According to Ken Hammon's canonical account of the shoot, chronicled in his essay 'This Has Buggered Your Plans for Conquering the Universe: The Making of Bad Taste',[12] *Roast of the Day* was a simple, single-joke short about a charity collector for famine relief who runs into a bunch of cannibals while doing a collection run. The hapless hero is cooked and eaten 'to relieve their famine' (Hammon 2001). It was always intended to be played for laughs, and was influenced by events in *The Texas Chain Saw Massacre* (1974). Hammon later recalled Tobe Hooper's notorious film 'really freaked us out. Pete loved it' (Pryor 2003: 31).

A slightly different account appears in Brian Sibley's Jackson biography, which suggests *Roast of the Day* was much closer to *Bad Taste* inasmuch as the cannibals turn out to be aliens in disguise (Sibley 2006: 71). But whatever the original premise of the film, *Roast of the Day* was not their first attempt at filmmaking. Jackson and various collaborators had shot a number of shorts over the years using his parents' 8mm camera, including one called *The Valley*, which was entered for a competition run by *Spot On*, a New Zealand children's television show. Another short film experiment was an action-oriented Bond spoof, with Jackson playing the hero. In 1981 Jackson and Hammon, who had met at Kapiti College in 1978, decided to shoot a vampire feature called *Curse of the Gravewalker*. The film was notable for its use of a wide-angle lens attachment bought by mail order, but it was never completed. 'After a year of this, sanity returned and we realised shooting a feature film on Super 8mm bordered on lunacy', wrote Hammon. His essay cheerfully relates these early escapades, which reads like a Boys Own adventure for the YouTube generation.

It is striking how much these young men's lives were steeped in the very stuff of movies, which found expression in their creative endeavours. Thus, *The Valley* featured stop-motion animation of the kind pioneered by Willis O'Brien in *King Kong* (1933) and later refined and popularised by Ray Harryhausen. These groundbreaking fantasy films inspired Jackson and his collaborators, as did the Bond franchise and, as Hammon reveals, Hammer horror films. As a consequence their productions are littered with filmic references. Just as an example, the hero of *Curse of the Gravewalker* was called Captain Eumig, a knowing wink at Hammon's Super 8mm projector of the same name, and the vampire leader was named Murnau after the director of *Nosferatu* (1922).

The extent of this immersion in film culture is evident from a couple of photographs of Jackson's bedroom in Sibley's biography. The first, circa 1979, reveals walls covered with posters for *Casablanca* (1942), *Dr No* (1962), *Goldfinger* (1964), *Thunderball* (1965), *Diamonds are Forever* (1971) and *Moonraker* (1979). The second picture Jackson describes as 'my bedroom in my early twenties, already starting to groan under the weight of geekdom books and videos', including a reproduction Oscar statuette (now, of course, replaced by the real thing). This provides a powerful insight into Jackson's obsessions, and the key to his success in making films that connect with fellow movie fans: '*I want to make movies that I'd like to watch …*' he told Sibley (2006: 551; emphasis in original).

Pre-production began around six months before principal photography started, according to Craig Smith, involving location scouting, prop building and special effects tests including the making of latex prostheses.[13] Jackson funded this from his wages at Wellington Newspapers, where he worked as a photolithographer on the *Evening Post*. Entirely self-taught, Jackson drew on magazine sources and books for technical information on creating special effects, like *Fangoria*, *Cinefex* and Tom Savini's indispensable handbook *Grande Illusions*, first published the year *Roast of the Day* began production.

Once underway, filming settled into a regular pattern. 'When Peter had scraped enough money to buy a roll of film we would convene on a Sunday at a location and shoot until the sun went down or we ran out of film', recalls Hammon. Over the course of production, Jackson's hometown of Pukerua Bay and the Gear Homestead were used as locations in addition to Makara, along with other local spots like Titahi Bay, Caroline Girdlestone's farm near Waikenae and even a darkroom and stairwell at Wellington Newspapers.

Demonstrating his DIY ingenuity within a very tight budget, Jackson constructed various pieces of equipment, including a camera dolly and tracks, a steadicam and a camera crane. Nearly all of the finished film was shot on Jackson's spring-wound 16mm Bolex camera, which allowed bursts of filming of up to two minutes before it needed another windup. The Bolex shot mute and a sound camera hired from the National Film Unit was used at one point, but the sync-sound was eventually discarded in favour of dubbing.

The cast were required to muck in with the shoot. 'If you were on set', recalls Smith, 'you might have to don an alien costume, run the camera, organise the catering, manage the

The self-taught Jackson and his homemade gun

physical effects or carry out any other task that was required – there was no union demarcation on the set of *Bad Taste*!'[14]

Jackson also fashioned a number of props, the most impressive being several of the weapons used in the film. As Tony Hiles' documentary *Good Taste Made Bad Taste* (1988) shows, these included a Stirling submachine gun and AK-47 rifles made from aluminium tubing, wood, cardboard and Fimo, complete with working bolt actions and magazine clips. The actors had to shake the weapons and blink rapidly to simulate a convincing firing action, and muzzle flashes were added using a double exposure technique.[15]

Roast of the Day was never fully scripted, and as a consequence 'there was a tendency to add details and for simple sequences to end up much more elaborate than planned' (Hammon 2001). Smith, chosen to play the central character Giles because, in his words, 'I was the only person Pete knew who had a background in amateur theatre!', recalls that Jackson 'had a clear vision of what he intended the film to be (though this changed from week to week!) but he was always open to suggestions'.[16] 'I kept shooting, shooting, every weekend' Jackson told Sibley, 'and then I'd go into the *Evening Post* to do my job all week long and I'd be sitting there, bored, thinking up ideas for the next weekend's filming. It was a classic "make it up as you go along" situation' (Sibley 2006: 74).

The most significant development was the addition of a daring SAS-style rescue mission to save Giles from the cannibals, who by now were aliens in human guise. According to Jackson, the 'SAS appearance in *Bad Taste* is directly linked to the siege of the Iranian Embassy in London, which occurred while we were making the movie' (Sibley 2006: 76).[17] Hammon notes the awkwardness of working this into the original plot for the joke to still work, and so it was decided the rescuers would themselves be 'part of the cannibal family and they staged the whole rescue because they like to play with their food!'. This necessitated additional cast members, and Jackson looked to some of those who had been working as crew on the film: Pete O'Herne, one of Jackson's boyhood friends, was recruited to the cast along with Mike Minett and Terry Potter, both of whom worked at Wellington Newspapers. 'We never got directions or anything', Minett later told Ian Pryor, 'we played ourselves right from the start. Just hammed it up' (2003: 44). At some stage during this period the film title changed briefly to *Sapien Alfresco* and then became *Giles' Big Day* (Sibley 2006: 76).

Over a year into shooting, Jackson hired editing equipment from the National Film Unit and cut the footage together. He was surprised to discover the unfinished film ran to around fifty minutes, and decided to expand the original idea to full feature length. Hammon suggests *The Evil Dead* influenced this decision, which they saw together at the Wellington Film Festival. He later wrote: 'its success had convinced Peter you could make money with a 16mm semi-amateur horror film.

We resolved to keep shooting … adding a ton of gore along the way.'

Sibley reveals the film at this stage had cost Jackson around $8,000, with a further contribution of $500 from Ken Hammon (2006: 84). With the decision to expand *Giles' Big Day* to full feature length came the realisation that additional funding was required, and Jackson wrote to the New Zealand Film Commission seeking investment of $7,000 in January 1985. The application was unsuccessful, but the correspondence reveals some interesting insights into Jackson's intentions. He maintained the film was 'science fiction but not in the connotations that most people have with that term', and although the 'horror is mainly in the gore field', 'potential "scariness"' was sacrificed 'for humour at an early stage' (quoted in Sibley 2006: 86). Moreover, the film was 'aimed directly at the *Monty Python/Animal House* punters, as well as the standard sci-fi/horror buff' (Sibley 2006: 87). Even at this relatively early stage in production the film was envisaged as a multi-genre pastiche with a good dose of comedy to attract a following among audiences most likely to be drawn to cult films.

The New Zealand Film Commission can be forgiven for not getting involved when Jackson first approached them because film is an inherently risky business, and the prospect of commercial failure increases when untested talent is involved. The Commission, set up in 1978, was tasked with promoting the production of New Zealand films, including by the direct investment of Lottery Board money. The ostensible aim may have been cultural, to support indigenous production so that New Zealand stories could be told. But investment had to be made 'with one eye firmly on the market', as Jim Booth had originally recommended in his proposal for establishing the Commission.[18] The economic benefits of a thriving local industry were also recognised and used to make the case for the Commission's role.

The Commission arrived on the scene at a time of resurgence in New Zealand filmmaking, with films like *Wild Man* and *Sleeping Dogs* (both 1977) attracting decent notices and large home audiences. Previously New Zealand barely had a film industry to speak of, and the Commission helped build on the momentum of this so-called 'New Wave' (Conrich & Davy 1997).

Production began to boom in the early 1980s at a time when tax shelter money was widely available. During this period Tony Hiles (Consultant Producer on *Bad Taste*) recalls that 'investors made more money if you hung the script on the wall and shot it out of focus',[19] testifying to the fact that quantity did not necessarily equate with quality. Once the tax shelter was finally closed in 1984, private investment in film dwindled to the point of non-existence, so that by August 1985, trade journalist Bruce Jesson reported what many in the industry believed: that New Zealand effectively had 'a state-run film industry … which operates from a government grant' (1985: 14). Worse still, local production was hit by a double-whammy: the effect of the tax shelter closure made funding harder while production costs had soared during the boom. These travails were not lost on Jackson, who later acknowledged it was 'pretty grim in the film industry' at the time (Sibley 2006: 92). *Bad Taste*, whose production spanned this difficult period, was entirely immune, in Tony Hiles' words,[20] because the filmmakers financed it personally, and cost inflation was not a significant factor.

Jackson continued to work on the project with his collaborators, while maintaining regular correspondence with the Commission, as recounted by Sibley. In his reply to the Commission's initial rebuff, Jackson offers his opinion of the film. He boldly claimed it 'has pace … good intelligent humour and the New Zealand locations give it a fresh look [that is] well away from American suburbia or log cabins' (in Sibley 2006:

91), qualities that correspond with those voiced subsequently in reviews and fan commentary. Elsewhere in the letter, in 'two pages of close argument' according to Sibley, Jackson draws comparisons between his film and others that have been welcomed 'in "art-house" cinemas' as much as 'in any video shop, showing that "sleazy gore films" can achieve a certain critical respect as well' (2006: 92). These include midnight movie favourites like *Night of the Living Dead* (1968), further evidence of Jackson's own cult aspirations.

The production faced another set back around the middle of 1985 when Craig Smith decided to withdraw. He no longer wanted to be associated with the violence and gore in the film, which offended against his newfound religious faith. As Jackson was determined to retain these elements ('without the "good bits" we'd have a real turkey on our hands', he wrote to Jim Booth at the Commission (Sibley 2006: 96)), Smith felt he had no choice but to leave.

This meant discarding the proposed ending, where Giles 'fights to the death with a stop-motion monster called the Botha Beast of Trom' before blowing up the alien spaceship with a bazooka (Hammon 2001). An elaborate sequence showing Pete O'Herne transforming into an alien was shot but discarded when the narrative was reworked to accommodate Smith's departure. Giles was killed off and the SAS impersonators became a 'special task force set up to monitor and react to any U.F.O. activities' (Jackson quoted in Sibley 2006: 98). In consequence the title had to change, so at Ken Hammon's suggestion *Giles' Big Day* became *Bad Taste*, with its double meaning describing 'the aesthetic qualities of the film' and 'the main plot device of a bunch of aliens with a taste for human meat' (Jackson quoted in Sibley 2006: 101). Jackson introduced a new character, Derek, whom he decided to play 'having literally run out of friends who could help' (Jackson quoted in Sibley 2006: 113). Terry Potter's temporary departure also necessitated his character's demise, but on his return Ozzy was reinstated, along with Giles when Smith later returned to the production, albeit in a much lower-key role as part of the sub-plot. Smith since feels his departure benefited the film: 'It forced Pete to completely retool the movie and it became a better film for it.'[21]

In August 1985 *Bad Taste* got its first ever piece of publicity with a brief description in the 'Short Ends' section of the trade paper *Onfilm*. Jackson submitted details of the production to 'provide a morale booster for everybody' involved (Sibley 2006:107), and they were duly printed. The piece mentions that Peter Usher and Dean Lawrie were involved in the shoot in addition to Jackson, Hammon, Smith, Minett and Potter, and describes the film as 'a 16mm feature for the video market', indicating rather modest aspirations. In addition to playing a 3rd Class Alien, Lawrie, introduced to the production by Terry Potter, donned the alien makeup to portray Lord Crumb. The cast of extras would eventually include many of Jackson's *Evening Post* colleagues as well as friends and family, and Doug Wren, another employee of Wellington Newspapers, played Lord Crumb in human form.

According to Sibley, this piece caught the eye of Costa Botes, a film critic on the *Dominion* newspaper, and when he met Jackson in 1986 on the set of *Worzel Gummidge Down Under* he expressed an interest in seeing the completed footage. The screening took place at the National Film Unit, and Graham McLean, another filmmaker, was also present. They were impressed by what they saw, and Botes later told Sibley that 'even though Peter was obviously struggling from a lack of resources, this guy was a very, very good filmmaker with an amazing facility for putting together action sequences' (quoted in Sibley 2006: 113).

'Word about the unknown filmmaker was spreading in the industry', notes Lindsay Shelton, the Commission's Marketing

Director at the time, a fact not lost on Jim Booth (2005: 89). In August 1986 Jackson got an opportunity to screen footage for Booth, who was impressed enough to ask Tony Hiles, a producer and director, for his assessment of the project as an investment proposition. Hiles was equally taken with what he saw, reporting presciently 'it could become a steady earning cult movie' (quoted in Sibley 2006: 119). This meant the film had the kind of market potential the Commission was looking for in its investments. 'I had never seen anything made in NZ like it before' Hiles later recalled, 'deeply laconic with a strong sense of hero hopelessness. Most of it did not take itself seriously, and it was all about having fun. I felt the fun could be infectious.'[22] Hiles volunteered to help produce the film on its way to completion, and this was enough for Booth to agree to invest, albeit mindful of Hiles' recommendation to drip-feed the project, keeping it 'reasonably lean and hungry' (quoted in Sibley 2006: 120–1). This also allowed Booth to make payments from his discretionary fund without seeking the approval of the full Commission board, evidence of the sort of rule-bending that later led Jackson to describe him fondly as 'a kind of bureaucratic pirate' (1997: 20). When Jackson received the first cheque for $5,000 he handed in his notice at work to devote his energies to the project fulltime.

Around this time Cameron Chittock joined the production, assisting Jackson with the special make-up effects. Later Hiles introduced a number of industry colleagues to the team, including Jamie Selkirk (editor), Michelle Scullion (composer), Caroline Girdlestone (art department), and Don Duncan (camera operator). Others joined once word got around, including Fran Walsh, Steven Sinclair, Bryce and Grant Campbell and Costa Botes.

With filming coming to an end a large injection of additional money was needed for post-production. This could not be invested from Booth's discretionary fund so a rough cut was screened for the full Commission board to gain their approval. David Gascoigne, then the Commission's chair, recalls that 'despite some nervousness, the board approved the post-production funding without significant dissension' (Sibley 2006: 130). As an act of caution the Commission did, however, require that its logo be removed from the beginning of the film.[23] It was only reinstated on DVD release, long after the film and its director had made their reputations.

Post-production comprised a number of elements: the original cast, coached by actor Peter Vere-Jones, added post-sync vocals (Hiles also asked Vere-Jones to supply Lord Crumb's voice following Doug Wren's death before the film was completed). The stereo soundtrack was completed with sound effects, Scullion's score and a song from each of the Remnants (Mike Minett's band) and Madlight (Terry Potter's group). Finally the 16mm print was blown up to 35mm so the film could be sold for theatrical release. The final cut had a whopping 2,302 shots, 'too many for the neg-matching computer and too many for the National Film Unit's laboratory grading computer', according to the press kit. The total cost of the film stood at 'just over $295,000' (Shelton 2005: 90), and it is no surprise to learn the majority went into post-production. The film was completed in late 1987, four years after it first began.

***

These, then, are the basic facts of the *Bad Taste* creation story according to the published record and embellished with additional interview material. The thing about creation stories is they recount only the grand flourishes of a founding cosmology, and tend not to get bogged down with the nitty-gritty detail of how, *precisely*, the Universe came into being. Such elliptical storytelling is essential given the sheer volume of potential detail, and so it is with standard 'making of' accounts of film production. Some accounts, like Ken Hammon's, painstakingly relay the minutiae of certain scenes or creative decisions, or detail how a particular shot or special effect was achieved. But rarely is the protracted and arcane process of making any given film laid down in its entirety, from start to finish. For one thing it would make for deadly dull reading.

'Making of' stories, like creation stories, are therefore highly selective in what they reveal, and an interesting question to ask is what has been included, and why? In other words, what elements are deemed by the teller to be of greatest interest and significance? In the case of *Bad Taste* a clear pattern emerges from the various published accounts. The elements given prominence are those most likely to foster cult interest in the film, by emphasising its marginal status (ultra-low budget, initiated by industry outsiders),[24] valorising its achievement in the face of adversity (funding set backs, cast departures),[25] identifying a maverick hero (Peter Jackson, the resourceful and determined 'Swiss army knife of creative ability')[26] and providing examples of its unorthodoxy (a short that grew to feature length, New Zealand Film Commission rule-bending, freely improvised narrative, and so on).

These types of 'making of' stories cannot in themselves make a cult hit, but they certainly aid the passage of a film into cult status by treating fans to an insider's view that favours the unconventional, encouraging their greater personal investment in the film. Within fan networks where trivia are traded and film reputations established and contested, these details are essential to the longevity of a film's cult profile, the common currency of devotional film appreciation.

3

THE BASTARDS HAVE LANDED

Bad Taste took its first bow on the world stage at the 41st Cannes Festival International du Film in May 1988. Much of the film's subsequent success stems from this headline-grabbing episode, which has become a vaunted part of *Bad Taste* folklore.

According to Lindsay Shelton, who oversaw sales and marketing at Cannes for the New Zealand Film Commission, *Bad Taste* was not the first Kiwi horror film to appear at the festival; that honour went to *Death Warmed Up* (1985), which provided a valuable lesson for *Bad Taste*: generate overseas success *before* release in the home market, which was notoriously dismissive of local films (2005: 77). 'In those days' states Shelton, 'it was accepted that publicity from overseas always helped create more interest in NZ, where the locals are impressed by success offshore.'[27]

Prior to the festival Shelton discussed the marketing campaign with Peter Jackson, who designed the sales brochure cover. It incorporated the image of Lord Crumb 'flipping the bird', which would become the main icon of the film, appear-

'Flipping the bird' in the New Zealand theatrical poster

ing on everything from poster art, video jackets and websites to t-shirts and other merchandise. 'I always liked the image of the alien jabbing his finger up' Jackson told his biographer (Sibley 2006: 137), and so, it would appear, did everyone else. It is a very strong image, full of delightful incongruity: the scowling alien, with a head like a fleshy skull, in a pinstripe suit, shirt and necktie holding an AK-47 rifle, topped off with an impudent finger brandished at the camera. It perfectly encapsulates the film's irreverent humour while providing visual cues for its fantasy and action elements.

Even before the market screenings Shelton managed to secure three pre-sales 'on the basis of the alien image and the synopsis', but these were postponed because Jackson 'didn't like the idea of his film being sold to people who hadn't seen it' (Shelton 2005: 90).

The spirit of the film's low-budget ingenuity and mischief making was carried through into the marketing campaign, described by Shelton as 'low-key, low-cost promotion' (ibid.). Tony Hiles, who accompanied Jackson to Cannes, later described the approach taken: 'We were inventive with our $112.50 marketing budget, which paid for 500 day-glo stickers with permanent adhesive. We stuck them on other people's posters, which pissed off a few. Complaints were made to Lindsay Shelton. We were naughty boys.'[28] 'I remember telling Peter and Tony not to stick stickers on private property' recalls Shelton, 'but I don't think they listened to me!'[29] In addition, the market screenings were advertised using 'about a hundred flyers that we tucked under windscreen wiper blades',[30] while another stunt involved a friend of Jackson's donning an alien mask and cavorting around the Boulevard de la Croisette.[31]

Bad Taste was the brazen upstart among the New Zealand films at the festival. '*The Navigator* (1988) was in competition and that raised the stakes for the NZ Film Commission' recollects Hiles. 'There were [five] other NZ films of standard quality at Cannes that year and I always saw them as book ended by *The Navigator* and *Bad Taste*. Extremes of style and content … But the pomp and ceremony amused me, so having the renegade film was much more fun than being either in the middle or on a lofty perch.'[32]

Quite what piqued the interest of those attending the market is hard to confirm after the fact, but the promotional campaign worked a treat. 'I was uncertain about how the market would respond to this film', says Shelton, 'because it was so different, and so "raw", from anything which I had shown to buyers before. It took only one screening for me to learn that the film was in demand.'[33]

The film had three market screenings in Cannes, all at the Olympia Cinema. According to Hiles: 'First there were a few in the audience, on the second there were a lot more (the journos liked it) and we had a full house on the final screening.'[34] Grace Carley, who went on to become the international sales agent for Jackson's next two features *Meet the Feebles* (1989) and *Braindead* (1992), attended a screening and recalls 'the loudest laughter came from Peter himself. I just loved [*Bad Taste*] to bits – it was so original and funny, and the exploding sheep just blew me away.'[35]

A flurry of sales quickly followed. Far from being a parochial curiosity, *Bad Taste* surprised seasoned experts by attracting a good deal of international interest. In this respect it lived up to Mark Kermode's conclusion on the universal appeal of horror: 'I can think of no other cinematic genre in which internationalism is so genuinely championed, and in which linguistic boundaries are so nimbly over-stepped' (1997: 64). The first territories to go were France, Italy, Spain, Netherlands, Belgium, Japan, Taiwan, Argentina, Paraguay, Uruguay, Mexico, Australia and the UK.[36] It went on to sell to many other countries, bringing the total, at the time of writing, to 57.[37] A sale was made to Canada but collapsed when the film was banned in Ontario for 'indignities to the human body' (see Shelton 2005: 92). At the end of the festival 'the film was theoretically in profit' because 'gross income from Cannes sales would equal the budget figure' (2005: 90).

Rights were also sold to Germany/Austria/Switzerland but the deal fell through because the distributor was worried about censorship. A German theatrical sale was not forthcoming until Astro Films picked up the rights a decade later (Shelton 2005: 92). The fact that *Bad Taste* was forced underground, appearing only at genre festivals and on bootleg videos, undoubtedly helped fuel its cult reputation in Germany.[38] Cult film fans like nothing more than a juicy bit of forbidden fruit to tempt them in.

During one of his trips to Germany to screen the film, Jackson agreed to allow Thomas Hartlage to put together and distribute an official *Bad Taste* soundtrack album. Hartlage first met Jackson in 1989 on a visit to New Zealand where the German was looking to set up a film project, 'a sort of road movie about the local New Zealand music pop/rock scene'.[39] A mutual friend in Wellington introduced Hartlage to Jackson, and he saw *Bad Taste* for the first time: 'I loved it. So bloody, but so funny at the same time. I just loved the dark humour.'[40]

When Jackson attended a festival in Hamburg in 1990 he stayed with Hartlage, and the soundtrack album idea was born. Scullion compiled the album at Radio New Zealand and Hartlage designed the sleeve, with a note from Jackson on the inside cover alongside images from the finished film and behind-the-scenes shots of the cast and crew. As an added bonus the album also contained a film poster. 'The film has steadily built up a following and letters began arriving "I love the music, where can I get the album?"', notes Jackson on the sleeve. 'I love the music too, and I realised that something ought to be done about it. Something has been done, and here it is.' Hartlage's QDK-Media label pressed over 1,500 picture-disc LPs in 1990, followed by around 1,000 CDs in 1991. They have long since sold out, distributed worldwide by German music distributor EFA and Hartlage also sold direct to customers by mail order. 'Most of our customers came from Holland, Japan, USA, England and many other countries where the movie was already an underground hit', recalls Hartlage. 'The movie was already famous on the gore scene so fans from all over the world were buying the soundtrack.'[41]

That image again on the QDK-Media soundtrack album cover

The only other country in which *Bad Taste* faced a censorship problem was Australia, although this did not affect the sales deal. It was banned for a period in Queensland before the local Board of Review was disbanded and the ruling was overturned (Pryor 2003: 56). A JVB VHS version was subsequently released, proudly proclaiming on the front jacket 'BANNED IN QUEEN-SLAND', using the controversy to help sell the film to daring audiences.[42] This was acknowledged in a posting to alt.cult-movies in July 1990, where an Australian discussant informs the online community 'I have seen videos for rent with the stamp "Banned in Queensland"– and naturally that makes them instantly more interesting', thereby broadcasting the controversy to a much wider audience.

Wherever possible Shelton tried to pursue theatrical sales for first release. 'Word of mouth and reviews were what this was about', he noted later, 'as was proven by *Bad Taste* start-ing with its theatrical screenings in the festivals.'[43] The strat-egy clearly paid off, capitalising on the buzz created at Cannes, which then flowed through subsequent marketing and PR in support of local theatrical releases and, crucially, video.

Despite better than expected sales, the lack of US interest was a blow because it was one of the indicators used by the New Zealand Film Commission to judge the success of its activities. Shelton tried hard to court American buyers: '*Bad Taste* was advertised [in the *Hollywood Reporter* Cannes special edition] because we thought we would try to attract "commercial" distributors who would not have otherwise considered NZ movies, and we chose the Reporter with an eye to the Americans.'[44] When no US distributors attended the screenings Shelton decided to approach them directly. An executive at New Line watched the first twenty minutes before declining to make a deal, and this was repeated with every distributor he visited. 'None was willing to release *Bad Taste* in cinemas', he later wrote, 'it was considered too extreme' (2005: 92).

The film had some festival screenings in the US, and a very limited theatrical run a few years later, but it was on video that it finally found its niche. Magnum Video released a VHS version of the film in 1989, using a quote on the front jacket from Tony Timpone, influential editor of *Fangoria* and *Gorezone* magazines, which established the film's cult credentials: 'Will do for video what ROCKY HORROR did for midnight shows.' According to Timpone, the quote was most likely one 'that I just gave to the PR people over the phone'.[45] VHS and later DVD releases have seen good, steady sales in the US, with renewed impetus following Jackson's *Lord of the Rings* success.

The French sale to André Koob of Eurogroup came with an added bonus. The distributor invited Jackson to present the film at the seventeenth Paris Festival of Fantasy and Science Fiction, held a month after Cannes in June 1988, where it won the Prix de Gore. Unfortunately this auspicious start was not followed by theatrical success in France. Shelton reports Koob's view that his decision to use original poster artwork, and not the iconic image of Lord Crumb flipping the bird, was behind the box office disappointment of the film's 40-print release (2005: 91). There was an upside: 'with fast growth in the home-video market, Koob was not out of pocket for long' (ibid.).

The French theatrical poster takes a different approach

Cannes was, by any standards, a resounding success for *Bad Taste* and this was translated into positive notices at home. Jonathan Dowling reported in his column for the *New Zealand Herald*: 'This year, New Zealand has much to be proud of. Not only do we have Vincent Ward's *The Navigator* in Official Competition, but a Kiwi flick of class and discernment is forcing its way through the cult movie market' (1988a). In another article Dowling explained *Bad Taste*'s success: 'It all comes down to knowing your market, and Jackson's self-described "black comedy splatter" film appeals directly to two distinct and popular film audiences – the exploitation and cult markets' (1988b).

As a consequence, on returning to New Zealand Tony Hiles secured funding from the New Zealand Film Commission Short Film Fund to make a documentary about *Bad Taste*. 'We were flavour of the month when we got back', Hiles recalls, 'and when I had the idea to trap the moment in time, funding was the least of my difficulties'.[46] The film, *Good Taste Made Bad Taste*, provides a remarkably rich source of information about the genesis of *Bad Taste*. It has a hallowed presence within fan circles, circulating via television screenings in countries like Germany and Britain, and, most recently, appearing as a special feature on a number of *Bad Taste* DVD releases.

Cannes was not in fact the first time *Bad Taste* was shown in a theatre. A review screening was organised for Mike Nicolaidi at a cinema in Palmerston North in April 1988. His review appeared in the respected trade journal *Variety* in June 1988, the film's first major critical notice. It was broadly positive, describing *Bad Taste* as 'Boy's Own Fodder Horror …an outstandingly awful, at times awfully brilliant, first feature from Peter Jackson'. Nicolaidi concluded by downplaying the film's chances of international theatrical success, noting its 'unevenness and tendency towards jokiness of particular Kiwi taste and sound may make it difficult to market theatrically overseas' (1988: 16).

In the event, *Bad Taste* fared better in a number of overseas markets than it did at home. It was premiered at the Wellington Film Festival, screening twice in July 1988 at the Embassy Theatre. Each programme started at 11pm, in the midnight movie slot, and the festival programme notes, written by Costa Botes, hailed the film as 'an extraordinary achievement'. 'Describing it as a low-budget spectacular in the tradition of *Dawn of the Dead* and *Re-Animator*', Botes continued, 'hardly does justice to the film's unique qualities.' Craig Smith recalls the cast was present for the premiere, describing the event as 'a fantastic occasion – a full house – and the film was very well received'.[47]

A week later *Bad Taste* featured as a 'Late Night Special' in the Auckland International Film Festival, billed in local press advertising as a 'low-low budget splatter extravaganza … Get together with your friends and be among the first to experience "Bad Taste"– we dare you!'

Although these festival appearances proved popular, the midnight movie release strategy adopted by the New Zealand distributor, marketing the film as a 'Kiwi Kult Klassic' and limiting it to late night showings,[48] yielded disappointing returns when the film went on wider release. The 1989 New Zealand Film Commission Annual Report drew a veil over the matter, simply stating that *Bad Taste* and two other films it supported (*Send a Gorilla* (1988) and *Illustrious Energy* (1987)) 'had limited releases' (New Zealand Film Commission 1989: 10). Ian Pryor reports the 'film won strong showings in the university town of Dunedin, but its overall New Zealand gross was nothing remarkable' (2003: 55–6). This offers proof, if such was needed, that there is no simple formula for creating a cult theatrical hit, even with the most promising ingredients.

Still, the New Zealand release drew mainly favourable press coverage, and *Bad Taste* avoided the fate of David Cronenberg's *Shivers* (1975), castigated on its home release for receiving Canadian government funding (see Mathijs 2003).[49] 'Do we mourn the fact that this gore-drenched epic held the New Zealand flag high at the recent Cannes Film Festival or do we celebrate?' wrote Colin Hogg in the *New Zealand Herald*. 'We celebrate' was his conclusion (1988). Stephen Ballantyne, writing in the *Dominion Sunday Times*, likened the film to 'a home movie inasmuch as it talks more directly to us than tidier constructions of the New Zealand film industry' (1988). He detected a refreshing difference in the way *Bad Taste* depicts New Zealand, setting it apart from 'most New Zealand films' that 'are made by liberal, middle-class minds': '*Bad Taste* operates entirely on enthusiasm unfettered by any sign of preachiness or moralising' (ibid.). The film was also nominated in no fewer than eight categories for the Listener Film and Television Awards in 1988, welcome recognition by the critical establishment (Cairns & Martin 1994: 69).

The film did respectable theatrical business in the UK, matching somewhat limited expectations, according to Joseph D'Morais of distributor Blue Dolphin.[50] The first public screening was held on 30 July 1989 at the Scala cinema in London as part of 'Shock Around the Clock 3', programmed by Stefan Jaworzyn, editor of *Shock Xpress*, and critic Alan Jones. Shock Around the Clock had developed over the previous two years as a popular showcase for weird and wonderful examples of extreme cinema, offering over twelve hours of back-to-back screenings for the hardiest and most dedicated aficionados. D'Morais showed the film to the programmers and they were suitably impressed. 'We thought it was cheap, nasty and pretty entertaining' recalls Jaworzyn, 'obviously a good choice for Shock Around the Clock. It's always nice to discover someone new and crazy making films like that – and almost single-handedly producing a film that lives up to its title!'[51]

Bad Taste was scheduled for a 1.30am screening and billed as the 'Surprise Feature'. Jaworzyn is 'pretty sure it was one of that year's festival hits ... though I remember a friend coming out and complaining that he couldn't understand the dialogue properly because of the New Zealand accents!'[52] Alan Jones concurs: 'Our audience went berserk for it, by this time it had a [reputation] anyway so they would. But it delivered everything a late 80s all-nighter crowd wanted.'[53] The screening note, written by Jaworzyn, suggests the film looks at first 'like a down under take on Troma's more wayward offerings, but *Bad Taste* has some moments of *genuine* humour as well as the more obvious barf bag brain-spilling, swill and AIDS cracks, not to mention a way with dizzying shakeycam work and some thoroughly vile "special" effects' (emphasis in original).

The film went on general release in September 1989, beginning with a run at the Prince Charles cinema near Leicester Square in London, another independent venue popular with seekers of the offbeat and obscure. A poster advertising the run was banned from the London Underground until the offending *digitus infamis* was removed, causing some mild, local controversy. According to D'Morais the film was booked solidly for around two years, playing all the major cities and attracting mainly young men and students.[54]

Bad Taste's theatrical release was greeted with mixed press reviews in the UK, although even very critical notices tended to acknowledge the film's energy and Jackson's accomplishment. Derek Malcolm, in *Midweek,* wrote the 'film has nothing to commend it but its foetid imagination', concluding that Jackson 'is a true loony, but you can't help admiring him' (1989: 28). Ann Totterdell of the *Financial Times* was less charitable, describing the film as 'slight and not very funny' with 'no plot or production values to distract you', although she concedes there 'is something admirable about *Bad Taste* being released at all, but it can only be recommended as a curiosity for the dedicated horror fan' (1989: 29). William Parente was equally dismissive in *The Scotsman*, describing the film as 'pretty unpleasant', but even he admitted 'Jackson is talented: in terms of limited resources, *Bad Taste* rivals John Carpenter's legendary debut with *Dark Star*' (1989: 3).

Anne Billson used her favourable review to make a point about the state of British filmmaking at the time: 'One cannot help feeling our own film industry will show signs of health only when its filmmakers forget good taste and start aiming for the jugular of the genre audience' (1989: 37). More fulsome praise came from Marshall Julius writing in *What's on in London*. He identified the film as 'an instant cult classic that boldly goes where no film has gone before' (1989: 71). And Brinley Hamer-Jones could barely contain his enthusiasm in the *Western Mail* (in a review coinciding with the film's run at the Chapter Cinema in Cardiff): 'And, if like me, you find yourself laughing at this unsavoury collection of bad jokes, gory special effects, and weird aliens, I'll see you in therapy' (1990: 2).

Six years after the film opened for theatrical business in the UK, *Bad Taste* was broadcast on terrestrial television as part of the BBC's Forbidden Cinema weekend in May 1995, during celebrations marking the centenary of cinema. There can be few more public proclamations of a film's transgressions than featuring in a season of banned, censored or controversial works on national television. Alex Cox, whose films, like *Repo Man* (1984), have solid cult reputations of their own, hosted the weekend of screenings. He was already known for bringing previously overlooked films to wider public attention through the popular BBC *Moviedrome* series, which he hosted until 1994. Yet *Bad Taste* was a curious inclusion because it was not banned, censored or particularly controversial in the UK. Doubtless it benefited from the exposure, adding credence to its reputation for low-budget outrageousness (helped further by the fact that *Good Taste Made Bad Taste* was screened immediately afterwards).

Lewis Davies, who as 'Lewman' runs the 'Official Peter

Jackson Fanclub' website 'The Bastards Have Landed' (TBHL) with friend Pete Gunter ('Reno'), was one viewer who took note. He recalls watching the broadcast aged 14. 'I was not prepared for what I was about to see. Never had I seen gore so vivid and comic like … I was in awe and quite disturbed at the same time!'[55] It left a lasting impression: 'I loved it! Jackson's wicked sense of humour, and unique characters really struck a chord with me. After studying how the film was made my appreciation for the film increased even more on the merits of its technical and fiscal achievements.' Davies began frequenting a Jackson fan site (*Heavenly Creatures* was also a favourite film of his). When the site closed in 1998 he decided to enlist Gunter's help in creating a new version, which became TBHL. They approached WingNut Films and were duly granted official status, marking the site out as a potent source of *genuine* insider information (which carries a premium in fan circles). The site, which has recorded a staggering seven million visits, features profiles of all Jackson's work, plus biographical details and news updates. The *Bad Taste* page offers a variety of resources including Ken Hammon's 'making of' essay, which was written specially for the site.

Every cult needs places of worship, and TBHL shapes up well to the task as cathedral and choir book, a space for communal reverence and contemplation along with approved materials for enlightenment. A number of other websites perform similar functions, and not only in the English language. Sites closely linked to TBHL include Kaihoro.de (Germany) and Good Taste (Poland).[56]

The Internet has proven to be more eclectic in its coverage of *Bad Taste* than the print media, featuring interviews with cast and crew that outnumber those conducted with Jackson (where in printed sources the reverse is true).[57] The most comprehensive website devoted exclusively to *Bad Taste* is run by Hamish Towgood, a New Zealander who first saw

A place for cult worship

the film with school friends when he was 13: 'It was a great experience, it introduced me into my love of film, and with that I owe a lot to it.'[58]

Towgood can still vividly recall his first viewing, which left him in shock: 'I hadn't seen brains exposed like that before. But I was strangely drawn to watch it again, [and] I enjoyed it.' So began a very significant relationship with the film, which he has seen over one hundred times: the very model of a cult film fanatic: 'I know it word for word, scene for scene. It's a film I always insist on putting on when someone says they have never seen it.' This desire to share his passion for the film, and encourage others to do likewise, prompted Towgood to develop 'The Ultimate Bad Taste' website.[59] He first contacted Pete O'Herne for an autograph after reading an interview with him on another website.[60] Through O'Herne, Towgood made contact with other cast members. The website developed out of 'a lot of photos and material' supplied by O'Herne, Craig Smith and Mike Minett, and was put together while Towgood was doing a web design course.[61] It has a global audience, although the majority of visitors are from the UK and Germany. As well as acting as an unofficial ambassador for *Bad Taste*, Towgood has helped to organise cast participation in fan events, and assisted with the development of the Australian region 4 DVD. 'Bad Taste [seems] to have latched onto me like a mosquito bite [and] it's nice to scratch.'[62]

* * *

Mike Nicolaidi was correct to point out the challenges in marketing Bad Taste for theatrical release, and Lindsay Shelton acknowledges the theatrical deals were 'frequently underwritten by video money'.[63] In fact the film was always expected to generate its greatest revenues on video, over a much longer period than is possible in the theatrical release window. Bad Taste's release in the late 1980s was timely for exploiting the growing home video market, which in less than a decade had matured into a multi-billion dollar business. It was, as John McCarty suggests, a golden age for splatter films, and the VCR 'contributed in no small way' (1992: ix).

Equally, Bad Taste benefited from the changing dynamics of cult film consumption inaugurated by video, beginning with VHS and continuing with laserdiscs and DVD. The home entertainment format liberated marginal films from their usual metropolitan hangouts, providing access to titles otherwise unavailable outside major towns and cities. Where choice was previously limited to the programming whims and brute economic realities of theatrical venues, video shops carried much wider stocks for rental or retail. Niche audiences, like horror fans, could also rely on well-developed mail order operations advertised in genre magazines and fanzines. Nowadays, of course, we have the 'long tail' of choice offered by Internet-based retailers and auction sites, catering to every taste and linking buyers to sellers across the globe.

Video also enabled fans to own physical copies of their favourite films, a welcome investment for those with a collector mentality (and creating, in the process, informal exchange networks allowing fans to share their enthusiasms by lending out films). Video was not the first home viewing format, having been preceded by the likes of 8mm, but it enabled the market to expand massively beyond hobbyists and technophiles, broadening the potential audience base for low-budget cult films so they could turn a profit.

The very act of viewing also changed with home video: pause, frame advance, rewind and fast forward options allow viewers to become acquainted with, and engrossed in, cinematic minutiae. Repeat viewing no longer involved turning up at the local flea pit every day to catch a film for the duration of its run (as Jackson had done for *The Man With the Golden Gun* (1974), which he saw four times in one week (Sibley 2006: 54)). VHS allowed audiences to scrutinise their favourite films whenever, and wherever, the fancy took them.

The coming of the laserdisc and DVD formats furnished new opportunities for indulging cultish preoccupations, with the prospect of high quality transfers, and better picture and sound fidelity for aesthetic purists, along with extra goodies like audio commentaries, featurettes and 'making of' documentaries for the cognoscenti. All of these features have been mobilised to *Bad Taste*'s advantage, so that by 2000, despite limited theatrical releases around the world, it had become 'the New Zealand Film Commission's most profitable investment' (Anon. 2000).

The limited edition two-disc Anchor Bay DVD, with its lenticular image of Lord Crumb on the front cover (the alien leader flips the bird as usual, but tilt the box and he gives a V for victory sign), provides a revealing example of how the format has been used to package and market *Bad Taste* as a cult object. Released in 2001, the back jacket makes a virtue of the DVD's limited run of 50,000 with a unique numbered sticker on each box. This conveys exclusivity, a desirable attribute for aficionados. The jacket also reprises Tony Timpone's marketing quote from the Magnum VHS, slyly updating it for the DVD format: 'WILL NOW DO FOR DVD WHAT "ROCKY HORROR" DID FOR MIDNIGHT SHOWS'. The inside cover clinches it with a selection of memorable quotes from the film, performing precisely the kind of textual dislocation that semiologist Umberto Eco argues is charac- teristic of cult films: 'in order to transform a work into a cult object one must be able to break, dislocate, unhinge it so that one can remember only parts of it, irrespective of their original relationship with the whole' (1987: 198).

**

Gorezone, the short-lived younger sibling of *Fangoria*, was the first genre publication to cover *Bad Taste*, in January 1989. The article, by Mario Cortini and Philip Nutman, was part of a 'Blood-drenched International Special' featuring pieces on the 'sordid cinema' of Jess Franco, as well as Italian horror filmmakers Dario Argento, Lucio Fulci and British shockers *Hellraiser II* and *The Lair of the White Worm* (both 1988).

Genre publications like *Gorezone* serve an agenda-setting function, argues Nathan Hunt, 'in which the magazine does not necessarily tell the reader what to think, but rather pro- vides fans with frameworks for discussion' (2003: 194). This seems a reasonable proposition, although difficult to substan- tiate without delving more deeply into the mechanics of opin- ion formation. Nonetheless, if we accept it for argument's sake then *Gorezone*'s role in establishing *Bad Taste*'s cult reputation has two related strands, which find expression in other genre publications of the period.[64] First and foremost, *Bad Taste* is made relevant to the readership's interests by being cast as a successor to well known genre favourites. *Gorezone*'s front cover announces 'BAD TASTE – This year's RE-ANIMATOR', a theme continued in Tony Timpone's edito-

The Anchor Bay DVD jacket offers exclusivity for fans

rial and the feature article, which likens Jackson's debut to *The Evil Dead* and credits Jackson as 'New Zealand's answer to Lucio Fulci' (Cortini & Nutman 1989: 23).

Also in tune with the readership's interests, the second distinctive feature of *Gorezone*'s coverage is the hyperbolic celebration of *Bad Taste*'s gore. Gore is what lingers in the mind longest after viewing splatter films; it is their defining characteristic, their *raison d'être* and it makes or breaks their reputations. To fans, well-executed gore effects can redeem an otherwise dire movie. Timpone's editorial sets the tone: 'Get ready for record amounts of evisceration and dismemberment from the land of the kiwi' (1989: 4). The theme is picked up by Cortini and Nutman, who describe *Bad Taste* as 'whacky ... and gory. *Very* gory' (1989: 20; emphasis in original). The film, they claim, 'does for brains what McDonald's did for hamburgers: spread 'em all over the place' (ibid.). Comedy does get a mention; Jackson admits to finding gore funny ('I see it all in Monty Python terms' he tells the writers, in an oft-repeated refrain). But in contrast to the film's coverage outside of genre publications, the magazine gives gore top billing above humour. This preoccupation with gory excess is rounded off with an inevitable discussion about the film's likely fate at the hands of local censors, which helps establish the oppositional nature of the film and its capacity to transgress screen entertainment standards.

Casting an eye over online fan discussions, this obsession with gore is also clearly evident. Thus, in the now defunct cultmoviesonline.com review site, 'gore' is the most common noun used in connection with *Bad Taste*, with 'gory' being the favoured adjective. Two examples illustrate this, from separate postings in March 2006: 'This movie has all the gore you could want. I strongly recommend you pick this up if you love movies full of gore', and 'Though overall this movie is a huge disappointment the only redeeming [sic] quality is the semi massive amounts of gore whitch [sic] is quite amusing.'[65]

Online fan commentary also abounds with the exchange of *Bad Taste* trivia that Hunt identifies as 'a form of cultural capital ... used to establish who is an insider and to declare others to be outsiders who do not have the right to participate within fandom' (2003: 186). The archive of the alt.cult-movies discussion group provides a fascinating record of *Bad Taste*'s emerging reputation, and trivia is key to this. The earliest posting to offer production details, from July 1990, provides some 'facts you may like (that IMO [in my opinion] give it the TRUE classic status it deserves)'. A list of five titbits of information follows, emphasising the production's ingenuity as evidence of its 'classic status'. Of course, fan trivia is not always accurate, despite the wealth of genuine information available online. Inaccuracies found on cultmovies.com include the assertion that the film was shot on a camcorder (from a posting in December 1998), filmed over a period of eight years (April 1999), sold to twenty-five countries in ten days (March 2000) and cost $11,000 (March 2004).[66] Note that these errors all serve to exaggerate and enhance those qualities admired by fans: the budget is smaller, the production lasted longer, and the film sold quicker than was the case in reality.

Online discussants frequently use rankings to locate *Bad Taste* within hierarchical lists (like best splatter film, best special effects and so on). In this way lengthy discussion threads develop where fans debate the relative merits of their favourite films, fleshing out their evaluations through comparison and exploring genealogical links between films. In tune with genre publications, *Bad Taste* is most closely associated in fan commentary with the *Evil Dead* series, George A. Romero's zombie films and *Re-Animator*. It never gets discussed within the context of New Zealand cinema; in these forums the film's national identity plays second fiddle to its genre affiliations. In popular discourse, as Lawrence McDonald notes, 'there has been a tendency to place [Jackson's films] outside the arena within which New Zealand film is discussed in cultural terms' (2005: 48). In this regard fan commentary differs from academic evaluations, like those that set *Bad Taste* within the tradition of 'Kiwi Gothic' (see, for example, Conrich (2005)).

The topics addressed in online fan commentary have changed over time, as one would expect given the film's longevity and the changing nature of Jackson's career, a reminder that cult reputations are never fixed. The earliest discussions involved spreading news of the film, which was still something of an unknown quantity in many countries. This invariably led to questions about how to get hold of video copies from those keen to see it for themselves. A discussant from Finland posted to alt.cult-movies in January 1992 asking 'does anyone know where I can order this film on video?' This led to a number of replies indicating how dif-

ficult it was to obtain copies. Such accounts of scarcity rein-
force the impression of *Bad Taste*'s marginality, adding to its
cultish aura.

The film is no longer difficult to get hold of, and knowledge of its existence, and Jackson's subsequent career, is
commonplace. *Bad Taste*'s reputation now rests on its gory
excess and low-budget ingenuity, with scarcity and marginality less prominent than before. This has led to the emer-
gence of a new element in online fan discussions in view
of Jackson's more recent critical and box office successes:
what we might term the authenticity of allegiance. This is
a variation on Hunt's conception of a trivia-informed fan
knowledge economy, whereby fans distinguish themselves
from their peers not by the detail or accuracy of their insider
information, but by claims to have discovered Jackson's tal-
ents through *Bad Taste* rather than his later work. In these
accounts, authentic fans were there from the start, recognising incipient talent, in contrast with the hordes of bandwagon
jumping, Johnny-come-latelys who found *Bad Taste* on the
back of Jackson's more widely acclaimed films. Thus, a post
by Air_Sabu on the *Bad Taste* IMDb discussion board entitled
'Who was aware of peter jackson/this movies existance [sic]
before LOTR' sparked a lengthy thread with the provocative
line that 'All y'all USA Marks act as if he was born in 2001.
This movie, along with meet the feebles and braindead [sic],
outranks ALL *beep* budget stuff he's done since.'

These contests around authenticity in fandom serve to
illustrate the 'competitive struggles' within cult circles (Hunt
2003: 198) while also reaffirming *Bad Taste*'s difference from
mainstream cinema (in the guise of Jackson's later work). A
common debate replayed endlessly in such discussions is
whether Jackson 'sold out' and betrayed his splatter roots
with his later films. It's a topic as futile as it is simplistic, for
it prompts far bigger questions about what exactly consti-

tutes mainstream and margins, two notoriously nebulous concepts. But it does highlight the opposition between these categories within the rhetoric of the fan community, which is significant because the oppositional positioning of cult audiences enables them 'to confer value upon both themselves and the films around which they congregate' (Jancovich *et al.* 2003: 2). In the next chapter we will continue with this theme by examining *Bad Taste*'s inner workings to see how the film operates in opposition to cinematic and social conventions.

4

MY FRIEND THE ASTRO-BASTARD: TIME FOR TALKIES

'The idea of interpreting films to mean whatever you wish them to mean is a pastime in which I've never taken much interest' (Peter Jackson, quoted in Sibley 2006: 539).

In a letter written to Jim Booth of the New Zealand Film Commission during *Bad Taste*'s production, Jackson described his limited aspirations for the film: 'Look, you know this is rubbish', he imagines telling the audience, 'and I know this is rubbish, so let's just unhook our brains and enjoy ourselves' (quoted in Sibley 2006: 91). Why, then, should we take the trouble to analyse *Bad Taste* in any great detail? Well for one thing, this self-effacing comment by the filmmaker cannot fully explain the esteem in which fans hold the film. But even if we accept the argument that *Bad Taste* is a silly, superficial work it is still appropriate to find out what makes it tick, and to divine the ways it connects with audiences, in order to account for its cult reputation. For as Bruce Kawin argues in his essay on cult phenomena, 'we don't go back to these films to say how silly they were; what we keep discovering is how terrific and even necessary they are to us. This deep appreciation is a serious province of value, almost a matter of devotion' (1991: 23).

* * *

On the face of it, *Bad Taste*'s eligibility for the cult hall of infamy seems plainly obvious. While commentators are often reluctant to specify firm inclusion criteria for cult cinema, most agree such films achieve their distinctive cultural position in terms of what they oppose. Thus Mark Jancovich, Antonio Lazaro Reboll, Julian Stringer and Andrew Willis suggest that cult cinema exists by means of a 'subcultural ideology' uniting certain filmmakers, films and audiences in their opposition to the 'mainstream' (2003: 1). More specifically, J. P. Telotte proposes that film cultists embrace 'a form that, in its very difference, transgresses, violates our sense of the reasonable. It crosses boundaries of time, custom, form and – many might add – good taste' (1991: 6). Already we can see, in just these two examples, how *Bad Taste* might usefully fit within a cult canon conceived along 'oppositional' lines. It is entirely plausible to imagine a subcultural connection between the fanboy filmmakers and similarly-minded members of the audience, while the film's lack of inhibitions poses a self-conscious affront to all 'sense of the reasonable'. In fact *Bad Taste* evidences the three characteristic markers of cult cinema distilled by Peter Hutchings from academic literature on the subject: their excess, potential for transgression and marginality (2003: 132). Gore films are by definition excessive, with the capacity to transgress commonly accepted standards of taste and thereby ensuring only a hardy minority will enjoy them. In *Bad Taste*'s case the film title is loaded with precisely these connotations.

Nevertheless, there are countless gore films that have not secured for themselves the 'cult classic' rubric, despite their excesses, transgressions and marginal appeal, which suggests additional factors are at play in explaining *Bad Taste*'s success. Chapter 2 described how the film was conceived with a non-mainstream audience in mind, confirming it as an example of what Kawin calls a 'programmatic' cult film, which 'sets out to be a cult film and often makes it appeal in terms of (or in terms of violating) shared values' (1991: 19). Furthermore, *Bad Taste* was actively marketed and distributed in ways designed to solicit cult status. But for the film to be *adopted* as such by its audience it has to offer them something different, some special qualities worthy of their devotion.

I contend that *Bad Taste*'s eligibility for adoption is greatly strengthened because it playfully challenges a number of cinematic as well as social conventions. The argument can be stated quite simply: there are equivalents of excess, transgression and marginality in the fabric of the film itself. Excessiveness is apparent in the way certain tendencies in horror movies are exaggerated in the service of genre parody (particularly the depiction of gore, whose stylistic excess is overblown to ludicrous proportions). And *Bad Taste* transgresses well-worn genre categories through pastiche, by lampooning science fiction, action and combat films alongside horror. Finally, the film evinces what Umberto Eco calls 'glorious ricketiness' (1987: 198) in its construction, a telltale sign of cult composition. Not only is it possible, as Eco describes, to conceive of the film after viewing 'as a disconnected series of images, of peaks, of visual icebergs' (1987: 198), but its unashamedly low-budget sensibility and cavalier attitude to narrative coherence ensure it occupies a place on the cinematic periphery. This marginal status is further assured because *Bad Taste* offers a distinctively Kiwi take on the gore film, locating itself outside the dominant national horror traditions that informed its making and constitute the main target of its parody (notably those of the US, Britain and Italy).

Bad Taste burst forth at a time in the 1980s when 'violent, gory, explicit, taboo-breaking and dangerous' horror films were spawning at an unprecedented rate (Balun 1989: 4), and the film's refreshing unconventionality no doubt helped it to stand out from other 'zero-budget, schlock gore video-tapes', which was Jackson's stated intention for the film (in a letter written to Jim Booth, quoted in Sibley 2006: 91). Non-conformity also enabled *Bad Taste* to court the attentions of potential cultists, particularly those knowledgeable viewers who derive pleasure from recognising its deliberate or inadvertent departures from cinematic norms. Such a reading strategy gives genre aficionados and cult movie junkies the opportunity to flex their filmic knowledge muscles (privately, or better still in discussion with other fans), and to express their affinity with the renegade filmmakers by colluding in the film's elevation to cult status (evidence, perhaps, of the shared 'subcultural ideology' described by Jancovich *et al.*).

In a related vein we also need to consider the richness, and particular flavour, of *Bad Taste*'s 'intertextual frames' (Eco 1987: 200), those narrative and iconographic elements that are familiar to audiences from preceding cultural traditions (including previous films) and are crucial to a film's transformation into a cult object. 'A cult movie', writes Eco, 'is the proof that, as literature comes from literature, cinema comes from cinema' (1987: 199). *Bad Taste* is a patchwork of intertextual allusions, lovingly pieced together from Jackson and his collaborators' expansive knowledge of popular genre cinema (including other cult films). 'I don't consciously go out looking for ideas' Jackson once told Barbara Cairns and Helen Martin, 'but anyone's a product of a lifetime's worth of influences and I'm the product of every movie I've ever seen' (1994: 79). Some of these references are explicit, as in the case of various film and television citations in the dialogue, and others are more oblique, formed from images or dialogue that are suggestive of certain moods, themes or episodes from other works. Fans find such intertextuality compelling because it taps into the reservoir of knowledge they hold dear, allowing those who would wish it to demonstrate their cultural (or even subcultural) connoisseurship.

THERE'S A LAUGH WITH EVERY DROP OF BLOOD [67]

In what follows I will expand on the foregoing discussion by examining *Bad Taste* from the perspective of its variegated comedy, a useful vantage point from which to survey the film's composition and the sensations and meanings it generates. Parody clearly figures prominently in the comedy throng, as does 'splatstick', a mode that brings together modern splatter techniques and silent-era physical gags. The analysis will also address the question of *Bad Taste*'s satirical content and its irreverence, which, although in tune with the oppositional politics of cult cinema, also play well in 'mainstream' comedies, a reminder that *Bad Taste* offers plenty of reassuringly conventional comic sustenance alongside its more challenging elements (which is one reason why the film appeals to people like Tony Hiles, who volunteered to act as consultant producer despite not being 'a fan of splatter flicks'[68]).

I. Parody

Whatever else we might think of *Bad Taste*, one thing is for sure: it is not a horror film. It may disport itself as such (horror has certainly been used as a marketing 'hook'), but that is because the genre, and more specifically the gore sub-genre, is the chief subject of its parody.

For argument's sake we might accept that *Bad Taste* shares many of the features of the contemporary horror film set out in Philip Brophy's seminal essay on 'horrality', whose publication in the mid-1980s coincided with *Bad Taste*'s production

period (for example, the 'act of showing over telling; the pho-
tographic image versus the realistic scene; the destruction of
the … body etc.' (1986). But in one key respect it is markedly
different: *Bad Taste*'s 'perverse sense of humour' (Brophy's
other key characteristic) is not counterpoised by anything in
the film likely to induce fear. Brophy suggests 'getting the
shit scared out of you – and loving it' (1986: 5) is the primary
pleasure of contemporary horror. But in its unconventional
approach there is nothing remotely scary about *Bad Taste*.

We can demonstrate this by considering the basic mechanics of cinematic fear. Alfred Hitchcock, who knew a thing or
two about it, famously described two forms of fear response:
terror and suspense (see Gottlieb 1995: 119). The former
relies on cinematic surprises (effects that make audiences
jump), while the latter involves a build up of tension resulting
from the audience's awareness of danger facing an oblivious
protagonist. *Bad Taste* induces neither terror nor suspense:
there are no jumpy surprises and none of the protagonists are
believably imperilled. In fact, the film's one-dimensional characterisation distances viewers from the threats posed to the
main characters to the point that we hardly care if they live
or die (if we're honest our only genuine concern is that if fate
decrees it they should meet their end in the most inventive
and spectacular fashion possible). As the author Stephen King
puts it, 'horror does not horrify unless the reader or viewer
has been personally touched' (1989: 26). In contrast, films
that have been most frequently associated with *Bad Taste*,
and that fit Brophy's specification of horrality more squarely
(like *Dawn of the Dead*, *The Evil Dead* and *Re-Animator*), all
contain moments designed to generate terror and suspense
with counterpoints of 'perverse' comedy.

These noteworthy horror antecedents also deal in dread,
the ice-cold-fingers-up-the-spine fear response neglected in
Hitchcock's scheme. Arguably it is dread (the fear of encoun-

tering something morbidly unpleasant, malevolent or threatening) that quickens the pulse in zombie movies, a sub-genre in which *Bad Taste* has occasionally been included (see, for example, Jamie Russell's zombie guide to zombie films, 2005: 159). We see it in the way characters, like Roger in *Dawn of the Dead*, recoil from the prospect of returning as one of the undead ('I don't want to be walking around like *that*! I'm gonna try not to come back'), and we can readily empathise. Zombification is hardly a beguiling prospect, lacking the seductive, sexual overtones of vampirism, and marked instead by the death of the spirit at the hand of corrupt flesh and the triumph of the mindless mob over individual free will. This is where, once again, *Bad Taste* diverges from the horror films with which it is most commonly associated. Zombie movies trade in their protagonists' fear of becoming one of the shuffling horde, whether by magic, demonic possession, infection or chemically-induced resurrection. But the aliens in *Bad Taste* have no interest in reviving their human prey, and why would they? The humans are nothing more than burger meat.[69]

The idea that *Bad Taste* is not a horror film should come as no surprise. Peter Jackson has been at pains to make the point ever since the film's Cannes debut. As he told Jonathan Dowling at the time: 'I'm not putting *Bad Taste* completely in [that] category, because it's not a horror film. There's nothing in it that's supposed to scare people' (1988b). Two years later Jackson admitted with heretical candour (in no less than the pages of *Fangoria*) that '*Bad Taste* [isn't] a horror film, it's not scary or anything' (in Balun 1990: 68). This idea did not elude Lawrence McDonald, writing in an article following the release of *Braindead*, who described Jackson as 'fundamentally a writer/director of comedy films' (2005: 49). By selling *Bad Taste* short as a horror title in print interviews, Jackson may have hoped to avoid disappointing viewers seeking conventional horror thrills. We can only guess at his other motives for steering the film away from the horror genre, despite its obvious advantages as a marketing category. Perhaps he felt a keen sense of filial responsibility to his parents, who encouraged and supported him through the production and may have been uncomfortable with the whiff of exploitation associated with horror. Or maybe it was a way of reassuring those at the New Zealand Film Commission who remained nervous about the use of public funds to bankroll the film. Whatever his motive, the message is clear: *Bad Taste* was intended as a tasteless bit of fun and emphatically *not* a video nasty.

* * *

For many of those who care to recall it, the most memorable part of the thirty-third episode of *Monty Python's Flying Circus* is the 'Cheese Shop' sketch, which finds John Cleese trying unsuccessfully 'to negotiate the vending of some cheesy comestibles'. But it was 'Sam Peckinpah's Salad Days', the skit that follows on from 'Cheese Shop', which most impressed Peter Jackson. 'That sketch did more to steer my sense of humour towards over-the-top bloodletting than any horror film ever did', he told his biographer (in Sibley 2006: 25). 'My splatter movies – *Bad Taste*, *Meet the Feebles* and *Braindead* – owe as much to Monty Python as they do to any other genre. It is about pushing humour to the limit of ludicrousness, the furthest and most absurd extreme imaginable – so extreme that the only possible response to it is to laugh because there is nothing else left to do!' (Jackson quoted in Sibley 2006: 26). What better inspiration for a cult movie than a cult television show?

Briefly, the sketch begins with Eric Idle, as critic Philip Jenkinson, introducing a clip from a fictitious film adaptation of

Julian Slade's 1950s stage musical *Salad Days* by director Sam Peckinpah. The excerpted scene shows Lionel (played by Michael Palin), a young chap in flannels, exchanging pleasantries with his pals as they frolic around a piano in the park. The frivolous mood is dashed when Lionel is accidentally struck in the face by a tennis ball. Blood gushes from an improbable wound, and one by one his chums are injured, dismembered and (in one unfortunate case) decapitated by similarly unlikely accidents. The sketch ends back in the studio where Jenkinson is dramatically gunned down as the final credits roll to the jaunty brass of the *Liberty Bell* theme tune.

A number of viewers were predictably shocked at the time of its first broadcast (in November 1972), despite a pre-emptive, tongue-in-cheek apology at the end of the episode ('The BBC would like to apologise to everyone in the world for that last item. It was disgusting and bad and thoroughly disobedient…' etc.). A BBC viewing panel reported objections ranging from complaints the sketch was 'rather too "horrific", "sick" and "gory", to protests that it was "repulsive", "distasteful" and "unnecessary"' (quoted in Hewison 1981: 22). Without wishing to labour the point, there are obvious parallels with *Bad Taste*'s *Grand Guignol* flourishes. When, for example, Derek fends off a pair of 3rd Class Aliens in a cliff-top skirmish, one of the hapless invaders has his arm torn off with the same unlikely ease as the 'disarming' of Lionel's friend Charles, played by Eric Idle.

The influence of 'Salad Days' can also be found in the way *Bad Taste* employs parody. The Python skit lampoons both Slade's play and Peckinpah's graphically violent work, and *Bad Taste* shares with 'Salad Days' a number of the methods for achieving parodic effects identified by Dan Harries, namely 'reiteration', 'extraneous inclusion', 'inversion', 'misdirection' and 'exaggeration' (2000: 37).

Reiteration is vital because it establishes a connection

between the parody and its target(s) through mimicry. 'Such anchoring', Harries tells us, 'is needed in order to ensure an established norm to play off of as well as to cue the viewers into a particular conventional viewing pattern' (2000: 54). A comical effect is achieved by mobilising readily identifiable characteristics of the subject and then confounding expectations by offering departures from them; parody, Geoff King notes, 'is often a matter of incongruity' (2002: 114). Reiteration forms the basis of all parodies, and through its outdoors setting, iconography and characterisation the 'Salad Days' sketch perfectly evokes the chirpy gentility of the play, while the bloody action is shot and edited using generous visual effects, montage and slow-motion techniques that reiterate Peckinpah's trademark style (to be a convincing parody we have to believe that Peckinpah could have filmed the scene, even though we know it not to be true).

There is also a form of extraneous inclusion in the incongruous merging of the *Salad Days* stage musical and Peckinpah's filmic violence, whereby foreign elements (in this case, bloody mayhem) are introduced into a conventional setting (the tranquil park setting familiar from the original play). This has the chief effect of inverting the play's light-hearted charm. Like reiteration, inversion is common to all parodies, and is 'a major means for up-ending established norms' (Harries 2000: 55).

Parodic incongruity can also be generated by an unexpected turn, through the technique of misdirection. In the 'Salad Days' sketch this effect is achieved when Lionel is struck in the face by a tennis ball (resulting is a nasty head wound); until that point the scene appeared to be developing along an entirely different course.

Finally, exaggeration ('one of parody's central methods of ironic transformation' (Harries 2000: 83)) works by magnifying or extending conventional elements to the point of absurdity. Evidence of this technique is found in the way the Monty Python team overplay the perky banality of the *Salad Days* characters ('What a simply super day', 'Gosh yes', 'Yes it's so, well, you know, sunny I mean'), and also in the egregious bloodshed, which goes much further than one might expect, even in a Peckinpah movie (and is variously described in the script as involving 'buckets of blood', an 'enormous pool of blood' and 'a volcanic quantity (really vast) of blood'; see Hewison 1981: 23).

The first point to note about the deployment of these techniques in *Bad Taste* is that the film is not a 'spoof' in the same sense as Mel Brooks' movies, or the work of Jim Abrahams and the Zucker brothers. Parody is just one of the comedy modes found in *Bad Taste*, and the incongruities at its heart stem from the filmmakers' enthusiastic commingling of cinematic influences and their desire to fully exploit the humorous potential of acts committed in dubious taste.

As previously noted, the primary subject of parody in *Bad Taste* is the horror/gore film, but even here some qualification is required. The statement is true to the extent that the film reiterates considerably more horror motifs than any other single genre through its visuals and soundtrack. To take a few examples, within the first five minutes of the film we meet 'Whitey' (played by Ken Hammon), a 3rd Class Alien in human form bearing an axe, who lumbers after Barry (Pete O'Herne) with the same implacable, laconic menace of an archetypal horror bogeyman. We also discover that Halloween is the date on the charity envelopes Giles (Craig Smith) is collecting in Kaihoro; and Castle Rock, the fictional setting of a number of Stephen King horror stories, is marked on a road sign consulted by Giles on his way to the town. Later, portents of death loom large when the action cuts between Barry, who passes a rotten sheep carcass on his way to the Alien HQ, and Giles who steps in roadkill while exploring Kaihoro's deserted streets (bringing to mind the upturned armadillo on the road-side that serves a similarly portentous function at the start of *The Texas Chain Saw Massacre*). And of course there's the frequent depiction of bloodletting in all its spurting glory, the *lingua franca* of the international horror genre.

While horror motifs run through *Bad Taste* like words in a stick of rock, the very first scene sets a more ambiguous tone, without reiterating horror in the straightforward fashion we might expect. The opening was added quite late on in the production, replacing a more conventional beginning. 'We needed a snappy set-up to launch the story', recalls consultant producer Tony Hiles. 'The film originally opened with Barry finding blood in the phone box, then the set-up unwound backwards too slowly'.[70]

The first shot, after the company credit, is an extreme close up of a photograph of Queen Elizabeth II in full regalia. Next we see an Ampex reel-to-reel tape recorder replaying a desperate exchange between a telephone operator and a man calling from Kaihoro, who recounts hearing '…this roaring noise and a big white light in the sky … and then … these … invaders started killing us!' The camera prowls over the Ampex, before cutting to a tracking shot of a shadowy man sat behind a desk, listening to the recording.

We are never introduced to him as such, but the man in silhouette is Coldfinger (played by Tony Hiles), a name reprised from an earlier Jackson short intended as a Bond spoof. The backlighting prevents us from clearly seeing his face, giving him a sinister presence that is further reinforced by sight of the prosthetic digit he uses to stop and rewind the tape machine. This staging, usually associated with archetypal baddies, is a red herring because Coldfinger is a character akin to 'M' from the Bond movies (the export script even calls him 'M').[71] He is not working for a SPECTRE-style crime syndicate: he has the ear of the Minister of Internal Affairs and a hotline to the Queen (as well as to the 'P.M.', 'MUM' and 'THE BOYS', according to the labels on his telephone). Though shadowy and digitally challenged, Coldfinger is on the side we are expected to cheer for.

Once we've heard the caller's untimely demise, Coldfinger asks for the Minister's opinion through a speakerphone. The Minister replies in a clipped, "old buffer voice": 'Call a full-scale invasion alert, sir. I'll phone the forces – fighters, frigates, footsloggers…'. Using an ornamental lighter, shaped like a hand, to spark up a cigarette attached to his prosthetic finger with a sticking plaster, Coldfinger intervenes before the Minister can get too carried away with his alliterative blustering. 'Perhaps that could all be a bit showy', he says. And after a pause to take a few puffs of his cigarette, Coldfinger concludes 'I think this is a job for *real* men', at which point he presses the button on his phone labelled 'THE BOYS' and the scene cuts to Barry in Kaihoro.

As presented the scene doesn't look or feel like anything appearing elsewhere in horror cinema. Viewers may justifiably ask what they have let themselves in for. Without clear genre markers (even reiterated ones), the audience is left to rifle through mental notes taken on previous cinematic outings to gain some purchase on the scene. Is it science fiction (an alien invasion is implied), or a spy movie? The opening's studied eccentricity bears the hallmarks of Monty Python, but there are also similarities with the genre-bending milieu of *The Avengers* (1961–69), or maybe Coldfinger is a warped version of Cowley and The Boys are *The Professionals* (1977–81). Of one thing we can be sure: the tragicomic desperation of the caller from Kaihoro and the incongruent figure of Coldfinger confound any expectation this might be a conventional horror film, or even a straightforward horror spoof.

We're on firmer ground once the action switches to Kaihoro. The zombie-like appearance of Whitey pursuing Barry helps orientate our genre bearings. But there's something amiss about the chase. Maybe it's the lack of volition, as neither seems in any particular hurry to get anywhere. Whether or not it was deliberate, their clumsy progress from the street to the fringe of the beach parodies the stock-in-trade horror pursuit by means of inversion, rendering it comical rather than suspenseful. The comical effect is heightened by Barry's half-hearted efforts at deterring the impending attack ('Just stop right there', he advises the alien, awkwardly raising his finger in an effort to strike a commanding tone).

Throughout this scene Barry is in radio contact with Derek, who gleefully informs his colleague 'the head shot's the only true stopper!', another zombie movie trope. Jamie Russell notes 'shoot 'em in the head' is a common refrain of *Dawn of the Dead*, and now a familiar part of zombie folklore (2005: 93). For those acquainted with the genre, this chipper Kiwi rendition of 'shoot 'em in the head' signals the coming bloodshed. It is the spectacle of eviscerated bodies that defines 'splatter' films (particularly shattered heads in zombie movies), thanks in part to Tom Savini's pioneering special make-up effects in *Dawn of the Dead*. Savini's craftsmanship in fashioning and combining prosthetics and make-up brought a new level of sophistication to the portrayal of gore on screen, placing it centre stage. Many of Savini's tricks are detailed in his popular fx manual *Grande Illusions*, which Jackson consulted when making *Bad Taste* (see Cortini & Nutman 1989: 23).

The ground is thus prepared for the first set-piece action, barely five minutes into the film. Barry fires three shots at close range, the last of which sends a mass of cerebral pulp flying into a rock pool behind the stricken alien. We are treated to a series of close-ups of Whitey's open top skull, in fulfilment of the grisly 'head shot' promise. There's no escaping the fact that Jackson's prosthetic alien looks fake, but

The head shot's the only true show-stopper

we are still ambushed by the graphic quality of the effects (thanks, in part, to the lacklustre chase that has brought us to this point, lowering our guard). We're just not used to seeing such close-ups, even in splatter movies. As John McCarty notes, gore effects 'are usually held in medium shot (and without editing) so as to make the audience wonder, *à la Grand Guignol*, how in hell the scene was accomplished without killing off the actor or actors involved' (1984: 2). But Jackson does not shy away from close-ups; in fact he actively indulges them without any attempt to preserve the illusion. That's the Monty Python influence again, pushing gore sequences to ludicrous extremes and spoofing through gross exaggeration.

Until now we've only known Derek as a voice over the radio. We get our first sight of him ogling the carnage on the beach through binoculars from a cliff-top vantage point. 'Oh Jeez', he sighs with drool running down his chin, 'I hope I'm not the poor bastard that's got to clean that up.' That rivulet of spittle indicates Derek's physical arousal by the violent spectacle of Whitey's death, telling us something about his dubious character. Drooling is a visual expression of desire (for food, thrills, whatever pushes your buttons), and is a classic 'Peeping Tom' reaction to vicarious stimulation. It provides further evidence of Derek's disturbing bloodlust, but also offers an interesting comment on the nature of splatter movie spectatorship that tips the film into self-parody. For Derek, like us, has only witnessed the action on the beach, not participated directly. His involuntary reaction is a reminder that the primary motive for watching splatter movies is to delight in gore, to experience the frisson of yucky pleasure (as William Paul notes, the 'perverse reversal' of gross-out movies is that they transform revulsion 'into a sought-after goal' (1994: 10)). His unsavoury response is a little joke at the expense of the splatter thrill seeker, for Derek (played by fanboy Peter Jackson) is one of us, if only we'd care to admit it.

Far from helping to unequivocally establish the style and mood of the film, *Bad Taste*'s pre-title set up, comprising the Coldfinger and Whitey scenes, invites ambivalent responses. Is this a horror film, science fiction, action, comedy, some combination, or none of the above? Does it follow in the tradition of Python or Romero? Is it mocking or teasing, shocking or pleasing? Is it badly made or made to be bad? Should we revel in its excesses, or be repelled? To its eternal credit none of these questions has a conclusive answer, but everyone who watches *Bad Taste* has to form an opinion of their own, and decide whether or not they like it. And in that difference the cult is born.

* * *

The multi-faceted nature of the parody continues after the main title appears. We are treated to a delightful example of extraneous inclusion when Derek produces his packed lunch from a holdall while hunting around for his bayonet

Delightful incongruities

and hammer in preparation for torturing Robert the alien. The same parodic effect is achieved in a later shot of Robert emerging from a ditch having escaped from Derek, decorously using a spoon to snack on Whitey's brains in a visual spoof of cannibal movies. A more complicated version of this technique is found in the transformation of the historic homestead into a spaceship (*à la The Rocky Horror Picture Show* (1975)). The old colonial property is a classic 'haunted house' location, and its revelation as an alien spaceship is both an example of misdirection (did you see it coming?) and extraneous inclusion.

A number of the codes associated with animated cartoons are also mobilised in *Bad Taste*, in another form of extraneous inclusion that achieves a parodic effect while also undermining the film's claims to realism. The punch-up between Barry and a mob of 3rd Class Aliens, after he is grabbed from behind and hauled inside a dilapidated garage, is shot in a live-action approximation of a cartoon fight. A crude montage of handheld camerawork involving canted shots, tilts and whip pans conveys the hidden action of the carefully masked mêlée. The sounds of punches and groans are heard as bits of wall fly off under the force of unseen blows and at one point Barry's head is shoved through a hole only to be dragged back inside. In keeping with the cartoon logic of this sequence Barry appears to be unscathed when he finally frees himself, despite the pummelling we imagine he's been subjected to. Derek's miraculous, Wile E. Coyote-like survival after falling from the cliff top functions along similar lines.

In another example, the comical image of Giles, mouth stuffed with an apple, marinating in a vat of liquid containing 'Reg's eleven secret herbs and spices', references the plight of victims of cartoon cannibals left to stew in giant cauldrons (as in, for example, the Bugs Bunny caper *Wackiki*

Cartoon allusions

Wabbit (1943)). And when Derek finally arrives at the historic homestead/alien spacecraft, he cuts his way into the building with a chainsaw, fashioning a hole in the exact shape of his body holding the power tool, just as Bugs Bunny might have done. The chainsaw is also put to good use when Derek cuts a perfectly circular hole in the floor above the room where Lord Crumb is standing, causing a piece of the ceiling to fall on the alien's head, in a variation on a corny cartoon sight gag.

'Quite often … film parodies spoof more than one established genre at a time', notes Dan Harries (2000: 33). Through a mish-mash of cinematic allusions, *Bad Taste*'s pastiche of genre codes further unsettles the idea the film is a straightforward parody of the horror genre. Other genres in the mix include science fiction, action films and the combat movie. The presence of aliens in the narrative is a science fiction plot device, and Lord Crumb's description of his planned invasion of Earth could have been penned by Douglas Adams, a Python collaborator and author of *The Hitchhiker's Guide to the Galaxy* (1979), sending up the genre with the same absurdist wit: 'Within a year the giant mincer will descend from the sky … the sun reflecting from its silver bits.' The lengthy mid-section shoot out during The Boys' assault on the Alien HQ is highly repetitive, exaggerating the monotonous gun battles of 1980s action films like *Commando* (1985). The action genre is evoked again with the shot of Ozzy's Rambo-like physique (Terry Potter, who plays Ozzy, was a body-builder) when he strips back to his vest-top, and there are similar echoes when Derek secures the loose flap of bone and skin on his skull by tightening a belt around his head like Rambo's bandana.[72] Finally, the stolid war film is spoofed when The Boys maintain the pretence of synchronising their watches, in true commando-raid style, despite only one of them having a functioning timepiece.

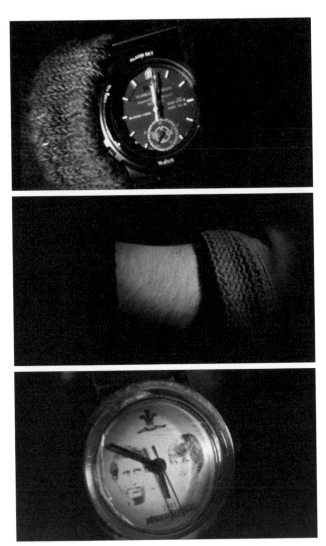

Combat movie parody

This pastiche also operates through the soundtrack, adding other influences along the way. Michelle Scullion's score encompasses familiar staples like soft rock and heavy metal (1980s horror movies), synthesised instrumentals (action films and science fiction), martial rhythms (combat films), doleful acoustic instrumentals (westerns) and rousing classical orchestration (typical of epic fantasies). This musical smorgasbord enables the parody to hit home with greater acuity by establishing an aural connection with the various genres traversed in the film.

In addition to these generic intertextual associations, *Bad Taste* also alludes to a number of specific films and television shows. In another example of extraneous inclusion, there's a reference to the much-lampooned closing sequence of *The Waltons* (1972–81) ('Goodnight John Boy'… and so on) when in a voiceover Lord Crumb bids his henchmen goodnight as the lights in the Alien HQ go out one by one. And *E.T.* (1982) is cast unceremoniously into the mix when Barry finds blood in a telephone call box and asks plaintively, 'Why can't aliens be friendly?' to which Derek replies, 'There's no glowing fingers on these bastards'. Similar passing references are made to *Star Trek* ('They don't need a base. They beam themselves down from their spaceship') and *Doctor Who* ('They might have come in a telephone box').

* * *

There is a happy fit between parody and cult film appreciation. They are mutually conducive, each requiring an awareness of film conventions among viewers. Knowledge of previous traditions (particularly those of the mainstream, ossified into popular genres) is essential for parody to work, because, as Harries points out, that is 'where its potential targets reside' (2000: 9). It is also necessary for the appreciation of nonconformity common to cult films. Little wonder, then, that parody often features prominently in films, like *Bad Taste*, celebrated as cult classics (think of, for example, *The Rocky Horror Picture Show* with its daring reworking of science fiction, horror, the musical and so on).

II. Splatstick

Along with Monty Python, *Bad Taste* owes a debt to the work of silent-era filmmakers like Buster Keaton, a parodist in his own right but also an arch exponent of slapstick. Jackson told his official biographer the films of Charlie Chaplin and Laurel and Hardy led him to Keaton, whom he admires for 'his eye for sight-gags and his immaculate sense of timing, particularly the split-second perfection of his stunt-work' (Sibley 2006: 17). It is qualities such as these that find expression in what Donato Totaro (2001) calls Jackson's 'gore gag comedy'.

The filmmaker's own preferred term is 'splatstick' (Sibley 2006: 143), a nifty enough neologism to describe the cohabitation of modern splatter techniques and older slapstick routines in the film, as well as their explicit blending in the gory sight gags for which *Bad Taste* is renowned.

In fact *Bad Taste* perfectly demonstrates how comfortable splatter and slapstick are as bedfellows, being well matched in terms of the demands they make on film structure and characterisation. On the matter of the former, it is possible to shoehorn the film into a classical three-act structure, as Barbara Cairns and Helen Martin have attempted (1994: 72), but this is rather beside the point because *Bad Taste*'s plot (such as it is) is elaborated through a succession of action-oriented set pieces, like the nested routines of slapstick comedies. Cairns and Martin judge this to be a weakness in the film's assembly, but it is also typical of splatter films, wherein 'plot serves mainly as a springboard for one violent/splattery/FX-laden set piece to the next' (McCarty 1992: viii).

Cairns and Martin are right to suggest the film 'rarely follows any of the conventions to do with characterisation' (1994: 73), as there is no great depth to the characters in *Bad Taste* and the story is not character-driven in any meaningful sense. Once again this break with dramatic convention has its roots in both slapstick and splatter traditions. The enjoyment of slapstick, Geoff King informs us, 'often depends on the establishment of distance from the comic figures who are not represented as "rounded" characters' (2002: 9), while inner conflict and character development are frequently sacrificed for external action in gore films. Bill Warren makes this point in his verdict on *The Evil Dead*, which could apply equally to *Bad Taste*: 'There isn't much time devoted to characterisation, but that doesn't matter much since the low-budget movie is so impressively cinematic' (2000: 8).

On occasion, what little back-story is given to the characters has the effect of confusing the narrative, rather than clarifying it. For example, Giles originally appeared in a scene with his boss, which explained why it was important for him to do well in his collection run in Kaihoro.[73] It was dropped, and the only vestige of this sub-plot is seen when Giles replaces his necktie with a fake clerical dog collar before entering the township. In the absence of any explanation Giles is liable to be judged a charlatan, and not a charity collector at all, making him a far less sympathetic character and placing his fate at the hands of the aliens in an altogether different context.

Similarly, while researching this book I was surprised to learn that Derek is the team leader of the Astro Investigation and Defence Service.[74] This fact is not at all clearly established within the narrative, and the team hierarchy is never made explicit. Frank (Mike Minett) is the most authoritative figure of all The Boys, seizing the initiative in his exchanges with teammates and issuing instructions ('Get in quietly, get out quietly' he tells Barry and Ozzy before the raid on the Alien HQ).[75] Still, the fact these narrative lacunae exist without unduly diminishing our enjoyment of the film is telling, a reminder that the establishment of character and story are of secondary importance to the visual set pieces in both splatter films and slapstick comedies.

The influence of silent-era cinema comes to the fore most conspicuously during Derek's cliff-top skirmish within the first half hour of the film, in a sequence of visual gags and choreographed action that is largely free of dialogue. It begins when Derek swaggers purposefully in the direction of the woods his assailants are likely to appear from and, in a classic pratfall, slips in a pile of sheep dung. Moments later he manages to narrowly escape injury from sledgehammer-wielding aliens by ducking and diving around a wire fence, with timing redolent of Keaton's nimble antics.

Other early cinema tropes in evidence include the classic mob chase when a group of aliens charge like a rush of gormless Keystone Kops after Barry, forcing him to take refuge in a shed (where, armed with a garden fork, he is prevented from surprising one of his pursuers because his jacket gets snared on a hook, in another nod to Keaton). Silent-era references find subtler expression when Derek recovers from his near-death plunge from the cliff top. Still dazed, he spies a blob of brain matter on the rocks and decides to return it from whence it came. He looks around sheepishly like Chaplin's Little Tramp before pushing it into his skull through a flap of skin and bone, and with the barest of smiles appears content with the result. Throughout the remainder of the film Derek has even fewer words of dialogue than before, the silent clown and laconic action hero evident in equal measures in his newly deranged persona.

By blending slapstick humour and splatter effects within a number of the film's major set pieces, Jackson and his col-

Silent clown and laconic action hero

laborators are able to exploit the comic potential of excess found in Monty Python while also pressing into service slapstick's 'relentless aggression against narcissism, vanity, snobbery and pride' (Neale & Krutnik 1990: 24). This assault on pretension sits very comfortably with what Pryor calls the 'Kiwi distrust of showing off for its own sake' (2003: 299). Nowhere is this better demonstrated than in the blood spurts that splash across the faces of our heroes, in a recurring visual motif. Essentially these are custard pie moments in the tradition of Mack Sennett's Keystone comedies, from *A Noise from the Deep* (1913) onwards.[76] The pie in the face, an act of mock violence deriving its comic force from sheer ludicrousness, is a very public form of humiliation. The facial target is critical in cinematic terms because it combines with neat visual economy both the action (the pie striking home) and the victim's reaction (which seals the audience's delight in the mischief-making). The same effect is achieved when Whitey's blood splashes onto Barry's face during their encounter on the beach (which is greeted by the sound of Derek chortling over the radio). This is not an

Custard pie moments

incidental spattering: it has been deliberately orchestrated for comic effect, achieved by means of a blowpipe filled with fake blood directed towards the actor's head. Shortly afterwards Derek gets a similarly bloody makeover having just extracted his bayonet from Robert the alien's foot ('I guess I should have expected that', he says ruefully). And poor Giles, squatting naked and helpless in the vat, takes a blood spurt full in the face when he dares to laugh at Robert after the alien accidentally slits his own throat. It is true that Frank and Ozzy escape unsullied in this way, but their come-uppance takes other forms (as when, for example, Frank is forced to eat alien vomit and Ozzy is shot and wounded in the leg). Although the good guys all survive and ultimately prevail, they are nonetheless fair game for the film's indiscriminate comedy, which never allows the heroes to get above themselves, a theme to which we will return in the next section.

The major splatstick set pieces in *Bad Taste* are distinguishable from the more mundane splatter effects that occur in the film (a machete in the head, for example) by their elaborate, gag-based construction. For example, when the recently deceased alien bearing a small claw hammer slumps onto Derek during the cliff-top fight, our hero is forced to push his gun through the alien's chest wound and out the other side to get a shot at another assailant. It is a grimly funny moment, our reaction to this defilement tempered by the absurdity of Derek's predicament and his unsentimental improvisation.

In another riotous example, which combines over-the-top gore, slapstick choreography and verbal humour, Ozzy uses his bare hands to decapitate an alien during the midnight raid on Lord Crumb's base. 'Jeez! They come to bits easy!' he mutters before drop-kicking the head out of an open window and delivering one of the film's most uproarious lines: 'The old magic's still there!'

'Jeez they come to bits easy!'

This routine leads into a fine example of gross-out comedy, which although not strictly a splatstick set piece (as no gore is involved) is nonetheless in keeping with the Pythonesque excesses found elsewhere. Frank, masquerading as an alien to spy on events inside the base, stands by helplessly as Robert pukes into a bowl with the same wince-inducing gusto as Mr Creosote in the Pythons' *The Meaning of Life* (1983). He begins to pick his way nervously through the crowd of aliens as one by one they sample the vomit, which turns out to be dinner ('Exquisite bouquet, Robert. Ah, aren't I lucky, I got a chunky bit!', says Lord Crumb). Frank is forced to take his turn and, in a comic reversal, appears to enjoy it, helping himself to a couple of extra gulps before handing it back.

The most elaborate splatstick sequence unfolds right at the end of the film, in a montage of shots charting Derek's passage through Lord Crumb's body. Having dropped onto the alien leader from above through a hole in the ceiling ('Suck on my spinning steel, shithead!'), Derek carves his way through the body with a chainsaw before finally emerging between Crumb's legs in a ghastly crimson tide of blood and offal. It's an extraordinary finale, once again leavened by humour: 'I'm born again!', quips Derek to camera, a literal reference to the messy act of parturition and a religious allusion intended as a dig at 'our fundamentalist friends'.[77]

In thinking about the deeper ramifications of humour in splatter films like *Dawn of the Dead*, Jamie Russell suggests it serves to make viewers 'even more aware of just how ridiculously vulnerable the flesh is' (2005: 95). But as these examples attest, the splatstick in *Bad Taste* operates on another level. The primary focus is not so much the human body and its frailty as the cluster of social taboos that surrounds our mortality and defines prevailing notions of good taste. In keeping with this theme, Barry Keith Grant notes a degree of amorality in Jackson's earliest films, founded on the way they 'mock the seriousness of violence and death' (2000: 21). Enjoyment of *Bad Taste* depends on how far the audience is prepared to laugh at strictures of social propriety associated with bodily defilement and death. The very fact that such extreme humour is not everyone's cup of tea is what gives *Bad Taste* the 'oppositional' cachet necessary for its adoption as a cult movie.

III. Satire

Given the nature of its storyline, *Bad Taste* can be read as a satire of the fast food industry and, by extension, American cultural imperialism. To this end Grant describes the film's 'vision of the invasion of New Zealand by fast food franchises', which, he argues, 'refers to the Americanisation of Kiwi dining culture that was fully underway while the film was being made' (1999: 10). Developing the theme further, Grant sees the depiction of pot-bellied aliens wearing denim jeans and shirts as testament 'to the conspicuous consumption characteristic of American culture' (ibid.). It's an intriguing thesis, but one that rests on there being some deliberate, satirical intent in this direction on the part of the filmmakers. There is no evidence this was the case, and Costa Botes has even suggested Jackson was a regular and avid consumer of fast food at the time he was making *Bad Taste*. When the filmmaker showed Botes photographs of his Cannes trip in 1988, 'they were full of pictures of McDonald's'. 'I asked why', recalls Botes, 'because, he said, that's where he ate. He didn't like foreign food' (2002). As for the aliens' appearance, Jackson used a cheap blue dye to give their shirts a cost-effective uniform look, and not for any sartorial significance; the jeans were simply what the cast happened to turn up in on the day.[78] On balance it seems safer to conclude the aliens are generic grotesques rather than American caricatures (Lord Crumb even has a distinctive British accent, voiced by New Zealand actor Peter Vere-Jones).

A stronger case can be made for the film's satirical handling of machismo, particularly those displays of manly bravado found in conventional action films. In a reflective moment Jackson once described *Bad Taste* as being about 'a bunch of blokes trying to be macho but failing' (Cairns & Martin

Cost effective uniforms

1994: 81). As such the film defies conventional expectations of heroic behaviour, while offering a tacit challenge to notions of Kiwi manliness. In fact the notable absence of women in the film (they are there, but hidden away as extras) is over-shadowed somewhat because the film's gender politics are far from favourable towards men. Michelle Scullion, the film's composer, suggests the lack of female images in the film is understandable because 'that's not what it's about. There is a piece of life in New Zealand that is boys out playing in the weekend. It's pre-sexual, little boy stuff' (quoted in Cairns & Martin 1994: 81).

Granted there are scenes aplenty of conventional action involving shootouts and fisticuffs ('boys out playing in the weekend'), but these are offset by moments of sardonic humour that undermine the whole heroic enterprise. In her review of *Jaws* (1975), Pauline Kael memorably described how Spielberg 'sets up bare-chested heroism as a joke and scores off it all through the movie' (1980: 196), a wonder-fully pithy and apposite description of the way the theme is handled in *Bad Taste*.

For starters, there is rich irony when Coldfinger tells the Minister of Internal Affairs the task of investigating events in Kaihoro is a 'job for real men'. While the archetypal *pakeha* (that is, white) Kiwi bloke is rugged, practical, down-to-earth and resourceful[79] (just the sort of qualities suited to seeing off an alien invasion), The Boys instead come across as inept, buffoonish and self-serving.

We first get the measure of this crack team when Barry flees from Whitey through the deserted streets of Kaihoro. His dif-fidence and reluctance to bear arms against the aliens suggest he would rather be pushing papers across a desk than tast-ing front line action, an impression reinforced later when he complains about having to don the unit's standard issue black fatigues ('I just wish we didn't have to wear all this crap'). And a suggestion of unmanly prissiness enters his character when he busies himself by mopping up bloodstains in the room where Kaihoro's butchered townsfolk are packed inside cardboard boxes ('somebody could get killed in here!' he observes without any hint of irony after slipping in the blood).

Meanwhile Frank and Ozzy, who, as 'the Bodie and Doyle of *Bad Taste*',[80] possess the outward appearance of more conventional action heroes, spend the first part of the film driving around rather aimlessly in their Ford Capri waiting for Derek and Barry to report back to them. At one point we find the pair parked by the roadside awaiting news, and Frank takes the opportunity to catch up on his overtime forms while Ozzy studies an issue of *Soldier of Fortune* magazine, the self-styled 'Journal of Professional Adventurers' and a favourite of military-obsessed fantasists. This is not the behaviour we have come to expect of *real men* of action; or rather it is not what we expect of our *cinematic* heroes. Perhaps the protagonists' depiction in *Bad Taste* is actually closer to what happens in mundane reality, with its boring interludes of pen pushing and fruitless escapism.

Killing time

Derek (the 'gung ho scientist') is the most unconventional member of the team, and the only one to successfully take the fight to the aliens by dispatching Lord Crumb and commandeering his spaceship. His most memorable line ('I'm a Derek, and Derek's don't run') was voted, without apparent irony, 'The Greatest Line in Kiwi Film' in November 2006 by viewers of TV One's flagship arts programme *Frontseat*, beating entries from more prestigious films like *Utu* (1983) and *Once Were Warriors* (1994).[81] The Film Jury who drew up the shortlist described it as a 'quintessentially Kiwi line' and 'an ordinary man's strong statement … the moment when you realise Derek is the hero of the film'.[82] Yet these are the very ideals subverted by Derek's portrayal as a deranged and querulous nerd, which are hardly qualities befitting a national folk hero. Nonetheless, they are clearly well-suited ingredients for a cult icon, judging by fans' adoration of the character.

It is significant that Derek is the outsider of the group, beloved only by the birds he keeps in an aviary ('Christ what a dork' says Frank at one point. 'How the hell did he ever get in this team?'). In a flagrant breach with classical war film convention, Derek's elevation to the status of superhuman avenger as the film closes carries an implicit critique of the male fighting unit represented by Frank, Ozzy and Barry, whose efforts are over-shadowed by the disturbed loner's exploits.

Despite these satirical undercurrents, *Bad Taste* also stands as a low-key celebration of masculine virtues like sporting prowess (as when Ozzy gleefully drop-kicks the alien's head out of a window) and 'mateship'. It is no coincidence the film was made by a group of friends; male banter sloshes around in the dialogue, written and performed with an acute ear for the ebb and flow of *bonhomie* and petty rivalries characteristic of the way close mates interact. It is tempting to see the onscreen relationships between The Boys as mirroring those found in their off-screen lives, and there are in-jokes to support this idea. For example, Frank instructs Ozzy to turn down the volume on the car stereo. 'Aw, that's elevator music for headbangers!' he continues, in a dig at the thumping music, which was contributed to the soundtrack by Terry Potter's band Madlight. Jackson added this line to poke 'fun at the "headbangers"' as he and Mike Minett were both fans of the Beatles.[83]

IV. Irreverence

Such was the depth of Jackson's feeling for the band, the Fab Four even make an appearance in *Bad Taste*, albeit as painted effigies. Jackson contemplated using some of their music on the soundtrack but settled instead for use of their images in Sgt Pepper outfits, which he hand painted and inserted into Derek's car. Their inclusion reflects the extent of Jackson's 'Beatlemania', as his biographer terms it (Sibley 2006: 79). Yet paradoxically, the way these images are employed in the film is distinctly irreverent, as if the filmmaker cannot resist the urge to make merry even at the expense of things he holds dear. When Derek swerves into an alien (played by Costa Botes) and cleaves him in two on the car bonnet, the twentieth century's most successful pop act are forced to bear witness to the splatter, with a couple of cheeky shots showing John Lennon (smiling warmly) and Paul McCartney (wide-eyed and boyish) looking on through the blood-drenched windscreen.

Let's be clear: this is not an attempt to satirise the Beatles phenomenon. As with the film's comic treatment of fast food, it is an example of *Bad Taste*'s cheerfully indiscriminate irreverence. Rather than the dissident intent of satire, irreverence pursues its targets merely for the sake of a laugh, and everything is fair game.

The lack of political guile in *Bad Taste* lends the film a

All you need is love

playful naivety, and its irreverent humour is definitely at the softer end of the subversive scale, like the mischief-making of an errant child. Jackson once told Cairns and Martin the film's humour is about 'doing naughty things like a naughty schoolboy teasing the girls' (1994: 75). By the same token there's nothing downbeat or exploitative about *Bad Taste*, despite the obvious scope for such dark moods in the story, and the film pointedly avoids the essential bleakness of its horror genre contemporaries (for example, *Evil Dead II* and *Hellraiser II*).

* * *

The irreverent tone is established right from the outset, in the pre-title sequence previously described, and here once again the influence of Monty Python can be felt. The cultural historian Robert Hewison notes the Python brand of humour was 'always funny about *something*, frequently about figures of authority' (1981: 8; emphasis in original). This is true of *Bad Taste*'s opening scenes, whose targets include the monarchy and New Zealand's colonial heritage (the very first visual is of a photograph of Queen Elizabeth II, presiding, as it were, over the state opening of a splatter movie), government (represented by the comically fulminating Minister of Internal Affairs) and their clandestine agents, the secret services (in the sinister guise of Coldfinger).

Consultant producer Tony Hiles makes a telling remark when he admits to being 'a fan of fun, of stretching credibility, being irreverent and being silly'.[84] Though the comedy may target authority figures and the establishment it is motivated by the pursuit of fun and not outright contempt for the status quo. This chimes with Grant's argument that cult films are not always as socially or culturally 'transgressive' as they at first appear, but may in fact be 'recuperative', reclaiming 'that which they seem to violate' (2000: 19).

The following example illustrates this. According to Ken Hammon, and since verified by Hiles, the filmmakers considered shooting a closing scene of The Boys receiving medals from the (then) New Zealand Prime Minister, David Lange, who was also revealed to be Derek's father. The PM was known to Hiles' partner through an oral history project she undertook with political party leaders in 1984, so there was a possibility, however remote, of the politician's participation. But the idea came to nothing: 'I seem to recall the idea got biffed', recalls Hiles, 'because it would look too much like a clip-on and not be integral to the story ... I think it was a fire-cracker of an idea – good while you have it, but dead in the water when it's over.'[85] But the fact they even entertained the idea suggests the filmmakers were happy for the film to include the most powerful political figure in New Zealand, a tacit endorsement of the political establishment even if the context of his appearance may have had the sort of irreverent undertones we saw in the treatment of the Beatles' effigies.

The victims of irreverence are not just the high and mighty. When, for example, Barry is pursued by Whitey, we hear Derek over the walkie-talkie: 'I think you'd better kill him Barry.' Barry demurs: 'Jeez, he could be Ministry of Works or something', allowing Derek to deliver the punch line: 'Nah, he's moving too fast.' The joke trades on the reputation for inefficiency of the Ministry of Works and Development, the government department responsible for building and main-taining public infrastructure like roads and power stations. The ministry was disestablished in 1988 following a review of the state sector under the reforming Labour government. The line can be enjoyed even without prior knowledge of the Ministry of Works, or the public sector reforms underway in New Zealand, because the slothful public worker is a com-mon enough stereotype for the joke to travel. As we saw in Chapter 3, *Bad Taste*'s review in *Variety* voiced doubts about the film's ability to travel overseas for fear it might be too parochial. This proved to be wrong because the Kiwi-themed dialogue frequently strikes a universal chord.

Two other topical references in the dialogue give the irrev-erent humour a local flavour, although their meaning may be more obscure to outsiders than the previous example. When Frank questions Derek over the radio about the alien inva-sion and asks rhetorically whether it is 'another false alarm like the Manners Street invasion alert', he is referring to a putative riot between Kiwi and US soldiers based in Wellington in 1943, triggered by the latter's racist attitude toward Maori servicemen. There is some question about whether the 'Battle of Manners Street', as it became known, ever took place, and Frank's comment seems likely to refer to the content of a revisionist article in the *Evening Post* (where Jackson worked), dating from December 1983 (during the film's production), dismissing the riot as 'largely legend' (in other words a false alarm, as reported in Belich 2001: 290). Later when Ozzy talks about a nuclear explosion 'on one of those Springbok warships', he is conflating left/liberal protests against Springbok rugby tours with the anti-nuclear demonstrations that led to US warships being banned from New Zealand waters. These were both major domestic political issues at the time, and Ozzy's unwitting (or witless) confusion offers a wry rebuff to international politics from the perspective of an ordinary Kiwi bloke.

The local flavour of the irreverence is also evident during a conversation about the alien invasion between Derek and Barry. 'They've wiped out a small town for starters. It's my guess they'll go onto something bigger next time' says Derek. 'Christchurch, Wellington…' he intones, listing major New Zealand cities. 'Auckland?', Barry interjects. 'Yeah, well that wouldn't be so bad' observes Derek, voicing the rivalry that exists between Jackson's home city of Wellington (New Zealand's political centre) and Auckland (the country's commercial heart), and which extends to sport and other aspects of civic pride.

Bad Taste also sullies the popular conception of New Zealand as a rural paradise. Much of the film is staged against a bucolic backdrop of rugged coastlines and hedge-trimmed fields, but this otherwise wholesome and reassuring image of 'God's own country'[86] is clearly at odds with the gory mayhem that Jackson and his collaborators orchestrate within its midst. This reaches its apogee in the closing stages of the film

Ovine collateral damage

when Frank fires off a rocket launcher at Lord Crumb just as Derek enters the room, so that the rocket passes harmlessly through the building before striking a startled sheep in the field beyond; the ovine collateral damage is a wickedly judged visual gag at the expense of the local celebrity export.

In a further elaboration, the film ridicules New Zealand's historic 'agrarian cult' of popular imagination, which valorises farmers as the 'backbone of the country' (Belich 2001: 152). On the radio to Frank and Ozzy, Derek begins to describe Robert, the 'intergalactic wanker' he has tethered on the cliff

Robert the alien: sort of human shaped

face. 'Well, I would describe him as sort of human-shaped. He's got jeans and a blue shirt on.' 'He's nabbed a bloody farmer!', quips Ozzy. After Derek observes there's something strange about his captive, 'Like he's got a screw loose or something', Ozzy gives a delighted cry of 'It is a bloody farmer!'

All of which, it has to be said, is just the sort of townie humour to be expected from a bunch of 'rowdy young hoons'[87] from Wellington.

EPILOGUE

'Family entertainment: bollocks! What they want is filth, people doing things to each other with chainsaws during tupperware parties, babysitters being stabbed with knitting needles by gay presidential candidates, vigilante groups strangling chickens, armed bands of theatre critics exterminating mutant goats – where's the fun in pictures? Oh well, there we are – here's the theme music. Goodnight' ('The End of the Film', *The Meaning of Life*, 1983)

There is no doubt that *Bad Taste* is popular, as much now as it ever was, and perhaps even more so given the uplift of interest in Jackson's career since *Lord of the Rings*. The film is well liked not just in terms of the number of people to have seen and enjoyed it, but also evidenced by the strength of individuals' attachment to it (in which case 'well liked' is probably too mild; loved and admired may be more appropriate). Cultish reverence finds expression in myriad ways: some personal, others communal. Of the latter, a good example is the online petition established by fans in 2006, imploring WingNut Films to make a sequel.[88] At the time of writing it has over 400 signatories, and the fan base is truly global judging by the rich variety of names listed.[89]

In a seminal statement on the nature of cult films, J. P. Telotte suggests that 'while many films aim at a very specific market ... it is clearly difficult to *design* a film for cult status' (1991:15; emphasis in original). Difficult maybe, but not impossible, as *Bad Taste* demonstrates. From the moment the filmmakers decided to expand the film to feature length, under the influence of midnight movie favourites like *The Evil Dead*, it was intended to have cult appeal. We can go further, citing letters written by Jackson to Jim Booth at the New Zealand Film Commission and quoted earlier: the film was deliberately crafted to include elements likely to find favour with that section of the audience drawn to outlandish or marginal movies. This was not the result of a radical artistic agenda, or a particular desire to reinvent the splatter film: it was a straightforward commercial judgement. Jackson's (and his collaborators') business instincts were acute, even at this early stage. He recognised the market potential of certain types of content, packaged in particular ways, which could be achieved relatively cheaply and within his modest means.

Success was not guaranteed, and many films made with the cult audience in mind have sunk without a trace. But *Bad Taste* did become, to use Tony Hiles' prescient phrase, a 'steady earning cult movie' because the filmmakers had talent, enthusiasm and the determination to deliver upon their intentions. More than that, they had the wherewithal, aided in no small part by investment from a government-backed organisation and with help from industry volunteers.

Making the film was only the start. The sales campaign, which began so successfully in Cannes thanks again to the New Zealand Film Commission, helped the product find audiences all over the world, building a momentum that carried through into the market place, where positive notices, strong word of mouth and sympathetic marketing were able to exploit the burgeoning potential of home video. The 'Kiwisms' that some feared might limit *Bad Taste*'s appeal outside New Zealand could not overpower the splatstick, with its visually rich blend of silent-era gags and modern gore effects. In other words, the film's local colour did not clash with the blood red Karo syrup sprayed liberally around the screen.

Despite the censorship hoopla that greeted it in several countries, *Bad Taste* probably has broader appeal than more conventional splatter films because it shies away from outright confrontation and horror. Its splatstick, multi-layered parody and cheerful irreverence has no more subversive intent than a 'naughty schoolboy', to use Jackson's own words. The closest the film comes to challenging our perception of the world is in satirising macho heroics, but the effect is somewhat overpowered by everything else that's going on. Grant notes that although *Bad Taste* appears to assault 'many cherished aspects of Kiwi culture', viewers can nonetheless 'enjoy laughing at themselves' (2000: 22). Ultimately it plays safe because there's a laugh with every drop of blood.

* * *

Bad Taste achieved the 'cult' accolade almost immediately. As early as 1990 Chas Balun, writing in *Fangoria*, described *Bad Taste* as 'a splat-happy black comedy' that 'quickly achieved cult status among the cognoscenti' (1990: 47). And the passage of time has witnessed the film's initial notoriety and novelty as a pioneering work of splatstick transform into *cult classic* status, a feat that could only be achieved with longevity. *Bad Taste* has inspired other young filmmakers, like Jonathan King, director of *Black Sheep* (2007), a film that 'owes a lot to Jackson's early offal oeuvre' according to one review,[90] and Jake West, the filmmaker behind *Evil Aliens* (2005), who explains why the film is special: 'when you watch [*Bad Taste*] as a young filmmaker you can see [Jackson] may not have had money, but he put love into it'.[91] Love that the film's legions of fans are happy to reciprocate.

Jackson's subsequent career has helped to keep the film in the public eye, but there was certainly nothing inevitable about his later successes. *Bad Taste* was no blueprint for *Lord of the Rings*, although it was an important step on that epic journey. Nonetheless, with the benefit of hindsight we can discern in *Bad Taste* a number of the defining characteristics of Jackson's body of work, notably the collaborative nature of his approach (he has co-scripted all of his subsequent films), a preoccupation with fantasy (which inflects even his more serious films, like *Heavenly Creatures*) and the privileging of special effects. But perhaps the primary factor linking all his work, from *Bad Taste* onwards, is the personal touch that Jackson the fan-boy brings to bear on every aspect of filmmaking, whether applied to low-budget schlock, mid-range specialty films or big-budget blockbusters.

Jackson's extraordinary success is certainly not the only reason *Bad Taste* has remained in the public eye. Ken Hammon's 'making of' essay, Tony Hiles' documentary, Hamish Towgood's website, Thomas Hartlage's soundtrack album, and Lewman and Reno's official fanclub site have all contributed to the communal pot of knowledge about the film (as, indeed, have others), keeping the folklore alive and helping to win new converts to the cause.

When all is said and done, though, we should be wary of unduly burdening *Bad Taste* with the weight of significance. It has a particular quality of levity, a knowingness that is unencumbered by pretension, which is in danger of being obscured by heavy-handed eulogising. In the end the key to understanding the film's true worth comes from answering a simple question, which Jackson and his collaborators understood well: Where's the fun in pictures? It is right there in *Bad Taste*, a raucous celebration of cinema as *entertainment*.

NOTES

1 http://www.innovate.org.nz/speakers-notes/harley.html.

2 Critic and author Tom Shone goes further, suggesting in his history of the blockbuster that 'Jackson's career path has proved *the exemplary one*, with Bryan Singer, Guillermo Del Toro, Darren Aronofsky, Ang Lee, Sam Raimi, Chris Nolan all mixing up low budget indie success with stints at the helm of the big studio blockbusters' (2005: 311; emphasis added).

3 'Kaihoro' is a linguistic joke, a conflation of Maori words that roughly translates as 'eat greedily'.

4 I am indebted to the BBFC for allowing me to interview Head of Policy Pete Johnson about the contents of the *Bad Taste* file. I was not permitted direct access to the file because the Board only makes them available to researchers twenty years after the date of the classification decision.

5 *Bad Taste* file, reference number AFF061908, BBFC.

6 Ibid.

7 Ibid.

8 In academic parlance, it provided a form of 'cultural capital' (or even 'subcultural capital') within the 'knowledge economy' of my student peer group (see Fiske 1992).

9 Craig Smith, email to the author, March 2007.

10 Ibid.

11 The short is described as a 'homemade 20 minute short' in *Celluloid Dreams: A Century of Film in New Zealand* (Churchman 1997: 75), which repeats the information provided in the original press pack ('BAD TASTE started as a 20-minute short…') but Jackson described it to Brian Sibley as 'a little ten-minute film' (2006: 70),

the same length that appears in Ken Hammon's 'making of' essay (2001).

12   Hammon originally wrote the essay for Jackson's official fan club website (http://tbhl.theonering.net/) in 2000 (published on the site in 2001), and it has since been reprinted in *Peter Jackson: From Gore to Mordor* (Woods 2005). It is so widely known within fan circles that Brian Sibley, Jackson's authorised biographer, felt able to skip many of the details safe in the knowledge that 'the full, in-tricate complexity' of *Bad Taste*'s production is 'already chronicled on a variety of internet web-sites' (2006: 73).

13   Craig Smith, email to the author, March 2007.

14   Ibid.

15   Filming also occurred at the Royal Tiger Range in Wellington, home of the Wellington Central Smallbore Rifle Club where Robin Griggs, who plays Reg the chef, was a member. Footage of live-round fir-ing was cut into the gun battle between the AIDS team and the aliens in the grounds of Gear Homestead.

16   Smith, ibid.

17   Operation Nimrod, as it was known, actually occurred in May 1980 although a television news image of the SAS storming the em-bassy appeared on the front cover of *Soldier of Fortune* magazine in October 1983, which Jackson may have seen at the time (the September 1981 issue appears in *Bad Taste*, read by Ozzy).

18   For a more detailed discussion of the Commission's early history see Waller (1996).

19   Tony Hiles, email to the author January 2007.

20   Tony Hiles, email to the author March 2007.

21   Craig Smith, email to the author, January 2007.

22   Tony Hiles, email to the author, January 2007.

23   Ibid.

24   In a letter to Jim Booth, Jackson described the cast and crew as 'amateur filmmakers that do not fit into the standard guidelines and film production methods established in this country' (quoted in Sibley 2006: 89).

25   Jeremy Clarke, reviewing the film in *Films and Filming* (September 1989) makes this point explicitly: 'As *film qua film*, *Bad Taste* is a remarkable achievement.'

26   Roy Battersby, quoted in Sibley (2006: 82).

27   Lindsay Shelton, email to the author, January 2007.

28   Tony Hiles, email to the author, January 2007.

29   Lindsay Shelton, email to the author, January 2007.

30   Tony Hiles, email to the author, January 2007.

31   A photograph of the alien carrying off a woman on the beachfront can be found on the cover of Shelton's book *The Selling of New Zealand Movies* (2005).

32   Tony Hiles, email to the author January 2007.

33   Lindsay Shelton, email to the author, January 2007.

34   Tony Hiles, email to the author January 2007.

35   Email to author, March 2007.

36   Lindsay Shelton, email to the author, November 2006.

37   Ibid.

38   The region 4 DVD includes a slideshow presented by Jackson at a festival held in Hamburg at the Alabama Theatre in 1990. Jackson made two visits to Germany during this period, testifying to the popularity of the film with local fans.

39   Thomas Hartlage, email to the author, March 2007.

40   Thomas Hartlage, email to the author, January 2007.

41   Ibid.

42   Ernest Mathijs (2003) describes how controversy can be used in a film's critical reception to construct its cult reputation, and the Queensland censorship decision is a good example of how such a strategy can be deliberately employed by canny marketers.

43   Lindsay Shelton, email to the author, March 2007.

44   Lindsay Shelton, email to the author, January 2007.

45   Tony Timpone, email to the author, March 2007.

46   Tony Hiles, email to the author, January 2007.

47   Craig Smith, email to the author, January 2007.

48   Ibid.

49   Tony Hiles recalls a television interview where the question of whether *Bad Taste* was an appropriate recipient of public money was raised, but this was the exception not the norm (email to the author, March 2007).

50   Joseph D'Morais, telephone interview with the author, January 2007.

51   Stefan Jaworzyn, email to the author, March 2007.

52   Ibid.

53   Alan Jones, email to the author, March 2007.

54   Joseph D'Morais, telephone interview with the author, January 2007.

55   Lewis Davies and Pete Gunter, email to the author, February 2007.

56 http://www.kaihoro.net/ and http://www.goodtaste.boo.pl.

57 See, for example, Badmovies.org (Pete O'Herne) and DVDactive. com (Craig Smith).

58 Hamish Towgood, email to the author, November 2006.

59 http://tbhl.theonering.net/badtaste/index.html.

60 http://www.badmovies.org/interviews/oherne/.

61 Hamish Towgood, email to the author, November 2006.

62 Ibid.

63 Lindsay Shelton, email to the author, March 2007.

64 For example, *Fangoria* (86) September 1989, 'The VideoEye of Dr Cyclops' review of *Bad Taste* on Magnum VHS.

65 http://www.cultmoviesonline.com as at February 2007.

66 Ibid. Dates of the postings are given in brackets.

67 This quote is taken from an interview with Joan Jackson (Peter Jackson's mother) in *Good Taste Made Bad Taste*.

68 Tony Hiles, email to the author, January 2007.

69 The lurching gait and blank expression of the 3rd Class Aliens probably explains why Russell included *Bad Taste* in his zombie filmography. Nonetheless he is mistaken in describing *Bad Taste* as 'a story of aliens turning the population of a small New Zealand town into blue denim-wearing zombies' (2005: 159).

70 Tony Hiles, email to the author, January 2007. The opening set-up was not to every reviewer's taste. Mike Nicolaidi, in a generally positive review for *Variety*, pointed to the 'badly set-up opening' as one of the film's faults (1988: 16).

71 Translators use an export script to produce dubbed or subtitled versions of a film. The British Film Institute library holds the version consulted by the author.

72 The original press pack even describes Giles' rescue as involving 'a series of Rambo-esque tactics'.

73 Craig Smith, email to the author, January 2007.

74 This was first revealed to me in an email from Mike Minett (February 2007) and subsequently confirmed by Ken Hammon (telephone interview with the author, March 2007).

75 The entry for *Bad Taste* in Steven Paul Davies' *A–Z of Cult Films and Film-makers* (2001) also makes the assumption that Frank is the leader, and, interestingly enough, so too does the documentary *Good Taste Bad Taste*, which describes Minett's role 'amongst the heroes' as 'leader of the pack'.

76 Anne Billson, reviewing *Bad Taste* in the *Sunday Correspondent*, describes how 'custard pie jokes are replaced by oozing entrails and brain matter' (1989: 37).

77 Craig Smith, email to the author, March 2007.

78 Craig Smith, email to the author, April 2007.

79 As exemplified in the writings of popular New Zealand author Barry Crump, whose novelised bloke had 'immense practical competence, disregard of material possessions, an ability to survive in tough conditions, a willingness to try anything, even if it was unconventional, and a rough-hewn wisdom and wry wit' (Belich 2001: 355).

80 Edwin Pouncey, *NME*, 23 September 1989.

81 See http://www.scoop.co.nz/stories/CU0611/S00223.htm

82 See http://www.the bigidea.co.nz/article.php?sid=3707&mode=thread&o

83 Mike Minett, email to the author, February 2007.

84 Tony Hiles, email to the author, January 2007.

85 Tony Hiles, email to the author, March 2007.

86 See Conrich & Davey (1997: 3) for a useful introduction to this popular epithet and Kiwi national identity, and again in Conrich's essay 'In God's Own Country: Open Spaces and the New Zealand Road Movie' (2000: 31–8).

87 The term used by Stephen Ballantyne to describe the filmmakers in his profile of *Bad Taste* (1988).

88 See http://www.petitiononline.com/bt2/petition.html.

89 Fans can take heart from the fact this proposition may not be too far-fetched. Sibley describes an aborted attempt to make two sequels back-to-back in 1993. 'In the event Jamboree [the project's codename] ... never got any further than a 22-page proposal and a detailed scenario. Even so, the idea lingers on' (2006: 268).

90 Russell Baillie, *New Zealand Herald*, 29 March 2007.

91 Jake West, interview with the author, March 2007.

BIBLIOGRAPHY

Anobile, R. J. (1975) *Buster Keaton's The General*. New York: Darien House.

Anon. (2000) 'Big Appetite for Bad Taste', *Onfilm*, November, 3.

Ballantyne, S. (1988) 'Jackson's home movie', *Dominion Sunday Times*, 24 July. Available at: http://tbhl.theonering.net/films/bad_taste_articles.html (accessed 23 September 2006).

Balun, C. (1989) *The Deep Red Horror Handbook*. New York: Fantaco Enterprises Inc.

____ (1990) 'The Feebles Pull Their Own Strings', *Fangoria*, 93, June, 45–9, 68.

Barratt, A. J. B. (2001) 'Video: Video Classification, British Law and Practice', in D. Jones (ed.) *Censorship: A World Encyclopedia*. London: Fitzroy Dearborn Publishers, 2570–2.

Bart, P. (2006) *BOFFO! How I Learned to Love the Blockbuster and Fear the Bomb*. New York: Hyperion.

Belich, J. (2001) *Paradise Reforged: A History of the New Zealanders from the 1880s to the Year 2000*. Honolulu: University of Hawaii Press.

Billson, A. (1989) 'Bad Taste', *Sunday Correspondent*, 17 September, 37.

Botes, C. (2002) *Made in New Zealand: The Cinema of Peter Jackson*. Available at: http://www.nzedge.com/features/ar-jackson.html (accessed 8 May 2002).

Bourdieu, P. (1986) *Distinction: A Social Critique of the Judgement of Taste*. London: Routledge.

Brophy, P. (1986) 'Horrality: The Textuality of Contemporary Horror Films', *Screen*, 27, 1, 2–13.

Cairns, B. and H. Martin (1994) *Shadows on the Wall: A Study of Seven New Zealand Feature Films*. Auckland: Longman Paul.

Churchman, G. B. (1997) *Celluloid Dreams: A Century of Film in New Zealand*. Wellington: IPL Books.

Conrich, I. and S. Davy (1997) *Views From the Edge of the World: New Zealand Film*. Nottingham: Kakapo Books.

Conrich, I. and D. Woods (2000) 'Introduction' in I. Conrich and D. Woods (eds) *New Zealand: A Pastoral Paradise? Studies in New Zealand Culture No. 6*. Nottingham: Kakapo Books, 8–10.

Conrich, I. (2000) 'In God's Own Country: Open Spaces and the New Zealand Road Movie' in I. Conrich and D. Woods (eds) *New Zealand: A Pastoral Paradise? Studies in New Zealand Culture No. 6*. Nottingham: Kakapo Books, 31–8.

_____ (2005) 'Kiwi Gothic: New Zealand's Cinema of a Perilous Paradise', in S. J. Schneider and T. Williams (eds) *Horror International*. Detroit: Wayne State University Press.

Corrigan, T. (1991) 'Film and the Culture of Cult', in J. P. Telotte (ed.) *The Cult Film Experience: Beyond all Reason*. Austin: University of Texas Press, 26–37.

Cortini, M. and P. Nutman (1989) 'Profile: Peter Jackson, Master of Bad Taste', *Gorezone*, 5, January, 20–3.

Creed, B. (2000) '*Bad Taste* and Antipodal Inversion: Peter Jackson's Colonial Suburbs', *Postcolonial Studies*, 3, 1, 61–8.

Davies, S. P. (2001) *A–Z of Cult Films and Filmmakers*. London: BT Batsford.

Dowling, J. (1988a) 'The Art of Bad Taste', *New Zealand Herald*, 17 May. Available at: http://tbhl.theonering.net/films/bad_taste_articles.html (accessed 14 September 2006).

_____ (1988b) 'Years of work in Bad Taste', *Evening Post*, 21 May. Available at: http://tbhl.theonering.net/films/bad_taste_articles.html (accessed 19 February 2007).

Eco, U. (1987) '*Casablanca*: Cult Movies and Intertextual Collage', in *Travels in Hyper-reality*. London: Picador, 197–211.

Elliott, M. A. (1918) 'The Frozen Meat Industry of New Zealand', *New Zealand Journal of Science and Technology*, May.

Fiske, J. (1992) 'The Cultural Economy of Fandom', in L. A. Lewis (ed.) *The Adoring Audience: Fan Culture and Popular Media*. London: Routledge, 30–49.

Gottlieb, S. (ed.) (1995) *Hitchcock on Hitchcock: Selected Writings and Interviews*. Berkeley: University of California Press.

Grant, B. K. (1999) *A Cultural Assault: The New Zealand Films of Peter Jackson*. Nottingham: Kakapo Books.

_____ (2000) 'Second Thoughts on Double Features: Revisiting the Cult Film', in X. Mendik and G. Harper (eds) *Unruly Pleasures: The Cult Film and its Critics*. Guildford: FAB Press, 15–27.

Hamer-Jones, B. (1990) '*Bad Taste*', *Western Mail*, 6 January, 2.

Hammon, K. (2001) *This Has Buggered Your Plans for Conquering the Universe: The Making of Bad Taste*. Available at: http://tbhl.theonering.net/films/bad_taste_kenessay.html (accessed 10 October 2006).

Harries, D. (2000) *Film Parody*. London: British Film Institute.

Hewison, R. (1981) *Monty Python: The Case Against*. London: Eyre Methuen.

Hills, M. (2002) *Fan Cultures*. London: Routledge.

____ (2005) *The Pleasures of Horror*. London: Continuum.

Hogg, C. (1988) 'Believe the name…', *New Zealand Herald*, 15 July. Available at: http://tbhl.theonering.net/films/bad_taste_articles.html (accessed 8 April 2007).

Hunt, N. (2003) 'The Importance of Trivia: Ownership, Exclusion and Authority in Science Fiction Fandom', in M. Jancovich, A. L. Reboll, J. Stringer and A. Willis (eds) *Defining Cult Movies: The Cultural Politics of Oppositional Taste*. Manchester: Manchester University Press,185–201.

Hutchings, P. (2003) 'The Argento Effect' in M. Jancovich, A. L. Reboll, J. Stringer and A. Willis (eds) *Defining Cult Movies: The Cultural Politics of Oppositional Taste*. Manchester: Manchester University Press,127–41.

Jackson, P. (1997) 'It Was Close Enough, Jim', *Onfilm*, November, 20.

Jancovich, M., A. L. Reboll, J. Stringer and A. Willis (2003) 'Introduction', in M. Jancovich, A. L. Reboll, J. Stringer and A. Willis (eds) *Defining Cult Movies: The Cultural Politics of Oppositional Taste*. Manchester: Manchester University Press, 1–13.

Jesson, B. (1985) 'Commission With a New (Bank) Role', *Onfilm*, August, 13–15.

Julius, M. (1989) '*Bad Taste*', *What's On In London*, 13–20 September, 71.

Kael, P. (1980) 'Notes on Evolving Heroes, Morals, Audiences', in *When the Lights Go Down*. London: Marion Boyars Ltd, 195–6.

Kawin, B. (1991) 'After Midnight', in J. P. Telotte (ed.) *The Cult Film Experience: Beyond all Reason*. Austin: University of Texas Press, 18–25.

Kermode, M. (1997) 'I Was a Teenage Horror Fan: Or, 'How I Learned to Stop Worrying and Love Linda Blair'', in M. Barker and J. Petley (eds.) *Ill Effects: The Media/Violence Debate*. London: Routledge, 57–66.

King, G. (2002) *Film Comedy*. London: Wallflower Press.

King, S. (1989) *Danse Macabre*. London: Futura Publications.

Malcolm, D. (1989) 'Bad Taste', *Midweek*, 14 September, 28.

Mathijs, E. (2003) 'The Making of a Cult Reputation: Topicality and Controversy in the Critical Reception of *Shivers*', in M. Jancovich, A. L. Reboll, J. Stringer and A. Willis (eds) *Defining Cult Movies: The Cultural Politics of Oppositional Taste*. Manchester: Manchester University Press, 109–26.

McCarty, J. (1984) *Splatter Movies: Breaking the Last Taboo of the Screen*. Bromley: Columbus Books.

_____ (1992) *The Official Splatter Movie Guide: Volume 2*. New York: St Martin's Press.

McDonald, L. (2005) 'A Critique of the Judgement of *Bad Taste* or Beyond *Braindead* Criticism: The Films of Peter Jackson', in P. A. Woods (ed.) *Peter Jackson: From Gore to Mordor*. London: Plexus, 47–57.

Neale, S. and F. Krutnik (1990) *Popular Film and Television Comedy*. London: Routledge.

New Zealand Film Commission (1989) *Report of the New Zealand Film Commission for the Year Ended 31 March 1989*. Wellington: New Zealand Film Commission.

Nicolaidi, M. (1988) '*Bad Taste*', *Variety*, 1 June, 16.

Parente, W. (1989) 'Splat falling flat', *Scotsman*, 16 September, 3.

Paul, W. (1994) *Laughing Screaming: Modern Hollywood Horror & Comedy*. New York: Columbia University Press.

Pryor, I. (2003) *Peter Jackson: From Prince of Splatter to Lord of the Rings*. Auckland: Random House New Zealand.

Russell, J. (2005) *Book of the Dead*. Godalming: FAB Press.

Savini, T. (1983) *Grande Illusions*. Charlotte: Morris.

Shelton, L. (2005) *The Selling of New Zealand Movies*. Wellington: Awa Press.

Shone, T. (2005) *Blockbuster: How the Jaws and Jedi Generation Turned Hollywood into a Boom-town*. London: Scribner.

Sibley, B. (2006) *Peter Jackson: A Film-maker's Journey*. London: HarperCollins Entertainment.

Telotte, J. P. (1991) 'The Nature of the Cult', in J. P. Telotte (ed.) *The Cult Film Experience: Beyond all Reason*. Austin: University of Texas Press, 5–17.

Thompson, J. O. (1981) *Complete and Utter Theory of the Grotesque*. London, British Film Institute.

Timpone, A. (1989) 'The United Nations of Splatter', *Gorezone*, 5, January, 4.

Totaro, D. (2001) *Your Mother Ate my Dog! Peter Jackson and Gore-Gag Comedy*. Available at: http://www.horschamp.qc.ca/new_offscreen/goregag.html (accessed 1 September 2001).

Totterdell, A. (1989) '*Bad Taste*', *Financial Times*, 14 September, 29.

Waller, G. A. (1991) 'Midnight Movies, 1980–1985: A Market Study', in J. P. Telotte (ed.) *The Cult Film Experience: Beyond all Reason*. Austin: University of Texas Press,167–86.

_____ (1996) 'The New Zealand Film Commission: Promoting an Industry, Forging a National Identity', *Historical Journal of Film, Radio and Television*. Available at: http://findarticles.com/p/articles/mi_m2584/is_n2_v16/ai_18897250 (accessed 7 September 2006).

Warren, B. (2000) *The Evil Dead Companion*. London: Titan Books.

Woods, P. A. (ed.) (2005) *Peter Jackson: From Gore to Mordor*. London: Plexus.

INDEX